FOLLOWING GOD'S PATH

A MEMOIR

FOLLOWING GOD'S PATH

A MEMOIR

JOHN KNOWLES

Following God's Path
Published by John Knowles
with Castle Publishing Ltd
New Zealand

© 2021 John Knowles

ISBN 978-0-473-58604-1 (Softcover)
ISBN 978-0-473-58605-8 (ePUB)
ISBN 978-0-473-58606-5 (Kindle)

Production & Typesetting:
Lizelle van Antwerpen & Andrew Killick
Castle Publishing Services
www.castlepublishing.co.nz

Cover design:
Paul Smith

CONTENTS

PREFACE

It has taken twenty-five years to complete the story told in *Following God's Path*. But it will continue on in eternity because, through Jesus, God has opened the way for us to have the certainty of a place with Him in heaven. The main purpose for writing was to bring together the stories of Lesley's life, my life and our life together. Primarily, this was done for our children and grandchildren, but with the hope that the book would also be enjoyed by our wider family and friends.

Some of the names of families and individuals have been changed to protect their identities.

I would like to give special thanks to Bernadette How for mentoring and encouraging me to go on with the writing process when I was ready to give up. To Rosemary Nisbet – my daughter – who very thoroughly read through the text and made necessary changes. And to Andrew Killick and his team at Castle, who have guided the publishing of the book and enhanced its quality. But, above all, God has been our supreme guide through this journey. Let us always give thanks to Him for everything.

CHAPTER 1

It was 1948. After a difficult six months at Drouin West in Victoria, Australia, our parents were moving to their second share-farming job at Willung, about seventy miles further east of Drouin West. They were offered this farm by a cousin of a friend at church.

The big black Packard rattled to a boiling halt. A cloud of steam issued from the front of the bus as Father lifted the side bonnet.

'She's boiling again. Get the water out Pete,' he said.

While Pete got the can of water, Father wrapped an old towel around the hot radiator cap. He then slowly unscrewed it. With great care, he poured the water into the thirsty, tired engine. Already she had endured a long twenty-year life as a small bus. Father bought her to transport local kids and us six boys to Sunday school.

We had packed and left our previous home to travel to this new life. Normally we would have all fitted quite comfortably, but this was the day of the big shift and what didn't go on the removal truck went in the Packard. This included the dogs, Monty and Hardy, and a young cat called Fairy.

Once the Packard cooled sufficiently we rattled off again, somewhat excited now as Mother told us it wasn't far to go. As we wound our way through the bush, little did we realise that in the next few years this same bush would become familiar territory to us. The engine noise quickened as we crested a long three-mile hill. Father applied the brakes as we turned off the main gravel road onto a sandy track only wide enough for one vehicle. For half a mile, our Packard wound its way through the trees as bracken rubbed along both sides trying to scratch the thick American paint from its body. As we came over a slight rise, a house was revealed sitting all naked and bare on the edge of the bush. It had a rusty roof and unpainted weatherboards. The toilet, a box-like shed with a flapping door, was fifty yards from the house. There was no fence or garden and the house looked all stark and lonely. This was to be our home.

Mother liked attractive things like houses with gardens and shrubs. This place didn't even try to look good. The nearest neighbour was a mile away. Shops were at Rosedale seven miles back along the winding, potholed road we came over. Three miles in the other direction, on an equally dusty road, was a small rural school.

We came to Willung as six school-age boys. Pete was the eldest and not long ago turned thirteen. He was boss of the tribe and at this stage of his life seemed quite aloof or reserved to me. David was eleven and nicknamed 'Dook' because of our children's book about an Indian boy called *The Doings of Dookie*. We all liked David. His was a rugged handsome face with a good crop of black wavy hair. Speed was his passion: whether it was running, riding his bike, or a horse, or later driving his car, he always wanted to go faster. Jim was ten and we called him 'Slim Jim,' because of his slender build. He had dark straight hair, brown eyes and an olive complexion. Graeme was the tidy boy in our family. A wave in his hair was nearly always neatly groomed, and his clothes seemed to keep clean even through the dirtiest of jobs. Uncle Wilbur, Father's younger brother, gave him the nickname of 'Squatter', but that didn't seem right to any of us boys. So, Graeme was always Graeme. I was seven when we arrived at Willung. At my birth, I was given the name John Winston. Mother told me later about my second name. Winston Churchill was at his finest hour with World War II in full swing when I was born. John 'Scon' was the nickname I was later given. Malcolm was the baby of the bunch. From a young age 'Blondie' was the nickname he was mostly called. He had pure blond hair until five or six years old, when his hair gradually darkened. The name still stuck.

The house was left like the farm, rundown and filthy. The kitchen cupboards were scrubbed clean before anything was put in them. All the floors were swept to remove the dust and bits of paper that littered them. That was Graeme's and my job. Mother said she would have preferred them mopped, but there was no time for that as the truck was already unloading. Jim lit the fire in the stove to boil some water. Things were quite hectic that day at Willung. Us lads wanted to explore, but all hands were needed to get sorted before darkness came. Bed was a welcome relief for everyone.

The farm required some hard work to clear the bracken and tussocks so more cows could be milked. From the back of the house was a one-hundred-and-eighty-degree view of the valley. A creek wound its way through the property to form the boundary for two sheep farms on the southern side. Merriman's Creek started twenty miles to the west and then gradually moved to a southerly direction for the next half of its journey. The creek ran in a valley where only the best land was cleared. The remainder was bush as far as the eye could see. To the north from the front of the house was a bush-covered hill. To a boy of seven, this bush would be pure adventure, but there were also some things to fear – snakes especially.

The farm covered an area of sixty acres of flat grassland with about twenty acres in tussock. The hill area of thirty acres had the longest boundary. This area was all covered in three feet high bracken ferns and clusters of gum trees. Many of the gums were dead and they littered the ground with their fallen wood. The main road ran along the short western boundary from our mailbox downhill to a bridge over the creek.

World War II had only ended three years before and this seemed the main reason the farm was in such disrepair. It would have been hard to find good people to look after a property like this one. Over the next few years Alex Ronalds, the new owner, and our family set about putting it in some sort of order. New fences needed to be built, ferns cut, rabbits dealt with, drains cleaned, tussocks grubbed, thistles cut, gravel carted for drives and ragwort roots salted. As well as all these extra jobs, there was the usual routine of milking cows, feeding pigs and calves, getting firewood and starting a garden. In every sense, this farm required a total makeover.

Without maintenance there was limited open grass for the dairy cows. Bracken fern and tussocks were encroaching on what was grassland for the forty-five cows and other stock. Rabbits lived in the bracken and destroyed a lot of the grass the cows needed. These bunnies jumped up everywhere. If we approached too close, we often heard two thumps as the lookout rabbit warned the others of an enemy coming. They scampered for their burrows. We could sometimes smell the rabbits when we got nearer to where they lived and see the fresh sandy earth where they had recently dug a burrow. Their smell of urine and dung was not too unpleasant; not like the pungent odour of pigs penned together, or cows in a yard. The smells were all so different. There were other more pleasant smells. I liked the aroma of a crushed eucalyptus leaf in the palm of my hand.

A path led from the back door downhill on a sandy track to a large cowshed with three silos right beside it. This cowshed was a hundred and fifty yards from the house. Further on and up the hill was a row of four pigsties. The farm had little fencing. There were fences around the bush edge of the property and along the two side boundaries, in urgent need of repair. In the summer, the creek was a place for adventure and fun. In the winter it sometimes flooded right across the low-lying pastures washing away trees and fences as it raced towards the sea, thirty miles away.

In our farmhouse was a large kitchen, a lounge, bathroom and three bedrooms. My parents used the bedroom off the lounge. The three youngest boys were in the room off the kitchen and the three eldest in the room off a short hallway that led from the back door to the kitchen. Each bedroom was furnished with beds, wardrobes, boxes and stuff. All the walls and ceilings were brown stained pine lining boards. Some of the rooms had very old lino on the floors, though all the bedrooms were bare floorboards. The bathroom was furnished with some shelves by the door, a galvanised iron bath on feet and a wash basin on a stand which was used by everyone until the water became too dirty and needed changing. A single cold tap over the bath was all we had.

A second-hand dining table and a six-foot long bench which Father made were placed in the kitchen. The length of the bench was the same length as the table and was a seat for some of us boys. He covered the tabletop with a new length of green lino, the same as we used on the kitchen floor. There were five wooden slatted back chairs with padded seats. Against the wall was an old enamel sink basin with a cold water tap which supplied water from the same pipe as the bathroom. The sink basin was set in a wooden benchtop with three cupboard doors underneath. It was about four feet long.

We put Mother's much-loved pedal organ and the lounge suite in the front room. Beside these were a formal dining table and six high-back wooden chairs and a dresser. The dresser held the dinner set, Mother's fine china tea set, white starched tablecloths, and matching napkins. These items were used only when visitors came or on Sunday nights for our evening meal. For our everyday meals we ate at the kitchen table and didn't bother with a cloth, to save washing and ironing.

The outside of our house, with its rusty iron roof, was grey weatherboard that had never seen paint. The front door opened to a veranda and a step to a dirt path leading to a broken picket gate. The gate was on the front boundary fence and was the only fence on any side of the house. Near the gate was an old-fashioned pink climbing rose which, like everything else, seemed as though it was uncared for since it was planted. But the incomparable scent, put in each beautiful flower by our amazing God, made visits to that part of the garden so memorable.

Not far from our back door was a laundry shed with broken wooden planks for a floor. Its woodfired copper, which held ten-gallons of water, was a round, seamlessly moulded U-shaped container, with a flat lip which ran around the top to help it fit snugly into its cast-iron fire box. The whole unit sat on six-inch high legs to keep it off the floor. A flue led the smoke out through the roof. The cold-water taps from a tank outside fed the copper and two concrete tubs nearby. These were on a stand about fifteen inches off the floor and there was a wringer in the centre partition of the two tubs. The wringer was used to get rid of the bulk of water from the clothes after they were washed. Ours had two white rubbery rollers three inches in diameter and fifteen inches long, fitted one above the other. A curved handle was used to turn the two rollers as they squeezed the water out of the clothes. Two of us usually were required for this job with one boy feeding the clothes into the rollers and the other turning the handle.

Most of the clothes were usually boiled in the copper with soap added. A strong stick was used to take the hot clothes out of the copper into one of the tubs to cool off before going through the wringer and into the other tub of cool rinsing water. We put them back through the wringer again before they were hung out on the clothesline. Mother waited two years before she purchased a petrol-driven washing machine with a wringer on the top. It cut the laborious washing time in half. However, there were some days when the motor wouldn't go. That wasted time, causing Mother considerable frustration.

The wastewater from the tubs trickled outside into a large puddle at the back of the shed. Concreting the floor and making the shed tidy, were at the top of Mother's priority for jobs that needed fixing. Father finally did it. We also dug a large hole out the back of the shed, filled it with rubble and covered the hole with the old boards. This helped the drainage from the back of the laundry shed.

Our bare house soon became liveable. From the time we moved in, there was a two-year plan to make changes. New lino was purchased for all the rooms. The walls were painted a pale cream and the ceilings in the kitchen and lounge were painted white. New tanks were put in to provide us with more water, though in the summer there was still never enough. There was no running hot water in the house and every morning the wood-burning stove in the kitchen was lit. It would be kept going all day and was the means of cooking and boiling water. There was a large two-gallon black iron kettle with a tap, and two smaller ones without taps that held another gallon and a half between them. These sat on the top of the stove. Soon after we moved in, new kitchen cupboards and a proper sink and bench space were installed. Much later, we put in a new stove which Mother loved and used to produce some wonderful dishes.

We would only bathe once a week and the hot water was carried by buckets from the copper in the laundry. The fire was lit under the copper each Saturday before dinner, or any other time when Mother decided to do the washing. Because of the shortage of water, two boys would share the same bath water.

A large woodpile was situated between the house and the loo. The wood was needed for the stove, copper, and the fire in the lounge. It became a constant job to keep the supply going. Winter was especially a problem when the wood was wet. The outside of the house was given three coats of a cream-coloured paint. Choice of colour was limited, but at least this protected the bare boards from the sun and rain. By the time our new shiny roof was installed, our house looked brand new.

When Alex Ronalds helped Father build a garage just outside the garden fence, they also decided to install a new loo. They put the new loo inside the garden fence, built a new door that could be shut from either side and laid a concrete path from the house to the loo. Mother was delighted with the finished job. The shorter distance proved a real blessing when one of us got the runs and needed to race to the loo. The convenience of a clear path, too, was a great improvement. The garage and the loo were both coated outside with black creosote which, for a few weeks stank of tar that even overpowered the smell from the loo.

We were without electricity for lighting until about two years before we left Willung. So, for most of our years there, we used candles or kerosene lamps in all the rooms. Filling them and keeping the glasses clean was another regular chore. If the wick of the lamp was turned too high, the glass became black with soot. A rag or newspaper was pushed in to clean the glass and get a better light.

One of our first outside jobs was to get water for the garden, the cowshed and for the pigs. Two men came and installed a new Southern Cross windmill by the creek. While this was being done, Father used Bobbin, the horse, to pull a single furrow plough to make a trench in which the galvanised pipe was buried. It was a straight line up to a new concrete tank at the top of the hill. The horse and plough were used for the first four hundred yards along a fence to the bottom of the hill. Then the trench needed to be dug by hand using a shovel and spade for fifty yards up to the brow of the hill. It was too steep to use the horse and plough on the hill, but they were used again for the seventy yards to the tank, down past the house to the cowshed and up to the pig pens. At last the job was completed with the water flowing freely from the windmill to the tank, from the tank to the garden and downhill to the cowshed and the pig pens.

The things mentioned above all took time to accomplish and we did most of them ourselves. Alex Ronalds helped pay for the jobs if he thought they improved the value of the property. He helped build the new garage, put in new fencing, and added the new bedroom on the front of the house which gave a fourth bedroom for guests. Alex owned a farm of his own at Gormandale, ten miles from where we lived. He used the same creek as we did. He was more than just a boss to Father. Over the years, he and his wife, Ivy, became much-loved friends of our whole family. Alex was an Elder and Sunday school teacher in the small country church we attended.

Willung was perfect in every way for us six boys. We had miles of room to roam freely, a good home and family, plenty of work to do, a good school to attend and a small church where we learnt more about Jesus and God the creator of us all. We saw God's handiwork by watching a chicken pecking its way out of a shell to become a living ball of yellow fluff. Sometimes we stood on the fence and watched the birth of a litter of pigs and counted them as they were born. Ten or twelve was a good number for a sow to feed all at once as she lay down and let them suckle. We watched a cow as it was ready to give birth. She looked for a place away by herself so she could protect her newborn. The new calf struggled for a few minutes while its mother licked it all over. Then it wobbled to its feet and tried to find his mother's teat. It was very special for me to see God's work as I grew to know more of His marvellous creation.

When I was born in May 1941, we were living in Bagdad about thirty-five miles north of Hobart, Tasmania. A shallow creek ran through the property. One hot summer's day, when Mother couldn't hear my brothers playing, she went out to look for them. To her surprise she found them all playing in the creek, completely naked, with their clothes on the bank of the creek in four separate heaps.

'And what do you think you're doing?' Mother asked.

David answered for all four and said, 'We're just playing bullfrogs.'

Do frogs wear clothes? I only learnt this story because Mother sometimes recounted it when we were sitting by the fire on a cold winter's evening. Malcolm and I always liked hearing about our older brother's mischief. It was in Bagdad that David killed his first snake by cutting it into inch-long segments with his axe. When my brothers told Mother about the chopped-up snake, she insisted they go and collect all the pieces with a bucket and spade so she could see it. Sure enough, they returned about fifteen minutes later with the grisly evidence. The snake was about ten inches long. David was six years old at the time and Father had taught him how to use a small axe, but only for cutting wood.

When I was two years old, Mother employed a girl to help look after us. There was an open fire in the lounge to warm the house. Over the fire were two metal bars for putting kettles or pots on for cooking or heating water. There was a large pot with a long, hollow, metal handle and on the opposite side a D-shaped handle to help carry the full pot. One day, the pot was full of boiling water and I managed to get the poker into the hole of the long handle. My weight was enough to push the inserted poker downwards, spilling all the scalding water onto the hearth which I somehow ended up sitting in. Pete told me that he and Mother had just finished milking the cow when they heard the awful screaming. They rushed to the house where Mother administered first aid and got me to hospital in Hobart. I was severely burnt on the legs and buttocks and was in intensive care for a few days. My total stay there was two weeks. How thankful I am that I have no memory of this incident.

All of us boys were Tasmanian born: Peter at St Helens in 1935 and David at Devonport in 1937. Our parents must have moved because Jim was born in Oatlands. Graeme was also born in Devonport where Mother's family lived. She had two younger, single sisters, Marion and Clare, who lived with their elderly parents. These two aunties came by train and stayed from time to time to help Mother, or to look after the other boys when she needed to go to hospital for another birth. I was born in Hobart in May 1941; Malcolm was born in the same nursing home in August 1942. As he was not doing well the doctors advised my parents to take him to a warmer climate. They chose Victoria.

We moved to Neerim South, Victoria, in late 1944. As the war was in progress, the ferry across to Melbourne was blacked out at night. Grandad and Grandma Knowles moved there before we arrived and bought a small farm they were living on. We stayed with them briefly until we rented a house further in the bush. Father secured a job at a local dairy factory, two-and-a-half miles from where we lived. He was discharged from the army on compassionate grounds in view of the family situation. By that time, the war was slowly grinding down to its conclusion.

Neerim South was a small farming community with a lot of timber in the bush close by. The rented house we lived in first was in a bush-clad valley with high gums on all the surrounding hills and half a mile to the main road. There was a small stream near the old house which was situated on ten acres of cleared, neglected paddocks and there was an extensive orchard at the back of the house. It was an unpainted weatherboard house with a huge blackwood tree at the front gate which kept the sunlight out.

One of my earliest memories of that place was Mother walking away from home in tears. I didn't know the reason why she left. She must have told Pete and David to take care of us younger boys. Father was away at work. I think she went to a friend's place. Jean Kent lived about a mile away in a nice house with a good outlook. It seemed hours before Mother returned, but until she did, there were some sad little faces in our house that day.

It was 1945 and World War II had recently ended. The people in the whole district were invited to the school by the armed forces for a celebration. We attended as a family and I suppose there were speeches and a parade of soldiers marching to the beat of drums. I have a vivid memory of a Spitfire which flew low over our school and made such a noise, it sent me running for shelter. I heard the plane coming back so I put my hands over my ears to block the roar, but I was determined to see the plane. I was just in time to watch it swoop down over the shelter shed and roar away while the people were all cheering and clapping. As the pilot pulled out of his dive, the tail of the plane was only a few feet from hitting the dome roof of the shelter shed. I later learned it was this type of aircraft that won a decisive air battle against Germany in the war. This was my first memory of seeing an aeroplane and hearing the thunderous roar of its motor.

We walked wherever we went until Father purchased an old Auburn utility. The car was driven by a gas producer because petrol was very scarce in those war years. A tin chimney was fitted on the side of the car, which was fed with charcoal to produce gas to fire the engine. At night-time, sparks came out of the exhaust. We used to watch from the back while sitting huddled in blankets as we chugged along. Petrol was not the only shortage. Tea, butter, sugar and meat were all rationed and we could only buy these foodstuffs if we had government coupons.

Not long after we came to Neerim South, Father bought a farm from Hector Cowden. When we arrived at the house, we had a panoramic view of the layout of the farm. Shady Creek was the main boundary which came out of a north-easterly direction and wound its way to the south-west. Grandad lived on the north side of the creek. Mr Caldwell farm was over the creek east of our house. His place was hidden by trees, but if the wind was blowing from the west, we could hear him working his sawmill. He had a bridge over the creek and used the road past our gate for access.

In spite of our fifteen dairy cows, an orchard with apples, plums, pears and quinces, ours was not a productive farm. There were some creek flats and on one of those paddocks, corn was grown for the cows. All the cows were hand-milked so any boys who could, were roped in for this job. Father still worked some of the time at the dairy factory. It must have been a huge financial struggle for our parents in those days, but they never complained. Our parents encouraged us to have animals or pets that we each called our own. On this farm, my calf was Buttercup. She was a Jersey calf with white and tan patches. When she grew and gave birth to her own calf, we started to milk Buttercup. In my opinion, Buttercup always gave the most and the best milk and it was nice on frosty mornings to have a large cup of hot Milo made from creamy cow's milk. The milk we got was all mixed up and put through a separator to take out the cream, which we sold to the butter factory.

We had a horse, a couple of goats that each gave birth to twins, a smelly old billy goat, some hens, two dogs and two cats. There was a big cherry-plum tree from which we picked many buckets of plums. Mother preserved as many as she could and made jam with the rest. Sometimes the plums were too green and sour but when they were fully ripened, they were delicious. Further away in the orchard, we had prune-plums which ripened a little later than the cherry-plum. They hung on the trees like big purple drops of coloured water when they were ready to be picked. Next to these plums were rows of three different varieties of apple trees.

Our grandparents ran a Sunday School in their home. One winter's day, we were all walking to Sunday School at Grandad's. I crawled along a log we used for a bridge to cross the creek. Our dog rushed past along the log and knocked me into the water. I fell six feet before hitting the water where I thrashed around until I managed to reach the hand David stretched out to me from the bank. My whole body was shaking from fright and cold. It took a while to catch my breath again, and we soon realised that we were still on the wrong side of the creek. When I saw Pete was holding onto our dog, I nervously crawled across the log again. By the time we reached Grandad's house I was freezing. My teeth wouldn't stop chattering. Mother made me take all my wet clothes off and stood me stark naked in front of the open fire while my clothes dried. I suppose I must have had a towel wrapped around me, but I only remember my embarrassment standing there starkers in front of the other boys and girls.

We were on the Neerim South farm when I turned six and started school. The school was built on the eastern side of the main road which ran through Neerim South township. The school yard covered about four acres which had a shelter shed, two outside toilets and some climbable trees. The local football field was over the eastern boundary fence. The yard had plenty of room for playing although it was mostly sloped downhill. The school buildings consisted of two large classrooms with enough desks to seat about fifty children in each room. There were four grades in each room and two grades per teacher. The headmaster, Mr Poletti, was one of the teachers for the seventh to eighth grade students and Pete and David were in the senior room while I was in the same room as Jim and Graeme.

I had difficulty getting my sums and spelling right. If I couldn't complete them on time, Miss Fairy, my teacher, used the edge of a wooden ruler across my knuckles or wrists. I used to try and stifle the sound of crying because that would only bring more harsh treatment. I hoped the cruel Fairy wouldn't see the tears that fell or come near me again until the lesson was over. I don't remember anything else about Miss Fairy, what the classroom was like or anything about the children who sat next to me. I was only interested in two things – avoiding what I thought was unfair punishment – and getting outside where I could climb some tall trees.

Sometimes the bigger boys helped us get into the middle of old truck tyres by holding the tyres upright. They held the tyres until three or four of us were each ensconced in our own tyres. David usually held my tyre and when someone called out, 'Get set. Go,' he gave me a good strong shove to start. We hurtled down the slope for thirty yards before coming to flat land which slowed us down a little for a further fifteen yards before we crashed into a wooden fence. There were times we fell out of the tyres part way through the race, but all who went racing enjoyed the thrill of being first to finish the race and the feeling of giddiness after.

The walk home from school was two and a half miles long. The road took us downhill, past the small hospital on the right and further down past the butter factory. We crossed over a bridge which was about fifteen feet above a shallow, slimy-green stream. The railway crossing was twenty-five yards past the bridge. Sometimes when crossing this line, some of my brothers put pennies or half penny coins on the track and waited to see them flattened as the train wheels went over them. Those mangled coins were our prized possessions for some years. We always waved to the driver who would blow his whistle and let out a cloud of steam to scare us.

Up from the bottom of the valley where the train went, began the longest and steepest hill climb of our homeward journey.

We walked down from the school about five hundred yards and I hated having to face this hill, especially on a hot summer's day. By the time we were on the top of the hill, we were only a quarter of the way home. Halfway home, there was an empty house on a rise above the road. There was an orchard at the back of the house.

One day, I was persuaded by my brothers to inspect the fruit at the orchard. Of course, we had to climb over the fence to reach the fruit. The wild birds had already destroyed some of the ripe plums and were flying out of the apple trees when we arrived. We were filling our school bags with the ripe fruit when we heard a man yelling from down the paddock on the other side of the road. We took off over the paddock and eventually joined the road further down the hill. I think that was the only time we went looking for a free feed at that property.

After church one Sunday when we were coming home along this same road the steering failed on our old car. Father yelled out to us to hang on tight. We careened off the road, through a pile of blackberries and over a small log before coming to a halt near the bottom of the gully. The man who had earlier chased us from the orchard, towed us out with his horse. Then Father tied the steering together with some wire and we carried on our journey home.

In 1946, we went to have Christmas with our relatives at Auntie Flo's house. On the way home, we met a terrible windstorm. We couldn't get along the road because a creek had flooded the low bridge. Father backed up about fifty yards, did a left turn which took us to a closed farm gate only a few yards from a large gum tree. Pete jumped from the back of the ute and opened the gate. Father drove through and stopped on the other side while Pete shut the gate and hurried to his seat in the back of the ute. Father moved the ute away just in time for us to see and hear a huge gum-tree branch come crashing down where we moved from, seconds before. This was a very near miss which could have caused death or injury to any or all of us. I got such a fright my whole body was shaking but I was able to mask it from my brothers because of the howling wind, and rain pouring on the canvas-covered roof. All of us were silent. Flashes of lightning were quickly followed by very loud claps of thunder. Father fought to keep the car from sliding off the muddy farm track he was forced to negotiate. We crawled along until we at last came to our farm where our car got stuck in the mud with our warm house in walking distance. It was still pouring with rain and darkness made things worse. Fortunately, there was an old shed about fifty yards away and we took shelter there for a couple of miserable hours. When the rain eased, we walked the last half mile home in the mud and darkness. It wasn't the happiest ending for a Christmas day.

In the morning, we discovered many fallen trees including one very tall, naked old gum we called the kookaburra tree. This tree was a landmark which stood alone in a corner of the paddock below our house. It was deprived of its bark and sometimes when the sun was setting, our old gum formed a magnificent silhouette against the brilliant colours of the sky. There was a dozen or so broken, hollow branches towards the top of the seventy-foot high tree which at its base measured seven feet across. Near the base was a blackened patch of charcoal where it had been scorched by a previous bushfire. I imagined in its past the tree was so beautiful and majestic standing in all its glory for at least two hundred years. Finally, it was the wind and lightning that revealed its secret by laying our tree on the ground and exposing its rotten core in a broken battered heap. No longer would we see the colourful rosellas going in and out of their hollow branch when they fed their young. No longer would we hear the proud kookaburras laughing every morning and evening when they stood with their strong open beaks pointing skywards while their boisterous laughter shattered the still morning air. No longer would we see baby kookaburras come from their nests, in the lower hollow branches and try to imitate the laughing sound their parents made. The tree, the birds and their cacophony of laughter were all destroyed by the storm.

It was Easter Saturday 1947. We picked, sorted, and packed several boxes of apples that we stored waiting to be sold. Father was planning another trip to Powell Town and he asked me to go with him. I wasn't sure I would be much help, but as I hadn't been before I was anxious to see what Powell Town was like. We travelled about twelve miles over a rough gravel road – mostly through dense bush – before we came to a sign, 'Powell Town', nailed to a tree. Round the next corner we saw ten new weatherboard houses on each side of the road. There was plenty of space around each house, though the bush behind them looked like it was determined to keep the sun away from them. The people who lived in the houses were newly arrived immigrant families wanting to start a new life in Australia. I later learnt that most of them were in refugee camps before coming by ships to Australia, and most of the ones we saw spoke German. The men worked in a timber mill nearby. The houses provided temporary accommodation, before they were trucked to another site when the work in Powell Town was finished.

This was my first time to hear some people speaking another language or speaking English with different accents. It was all so strange to me, but Father was able to communicate the price of the apples to them. Many of them knew Father because of his previous visits and while some were away that day, those that were home were delighted to have some fresh fruit delivered. Father gave everyone two or three more apples than they paid for.

With all the apples sold, Father suggested we stop for lunch at a nice spot on the other end of town.

'Let's go there, you can get the lunch bag out when we stop,' Father said.

He turned off the road beside a gum tree and we sat on the running board and he gave thanks for the food and the good trip so far. I was eating my sandwich and looking back along the road, when a small boy came out and slowly shuffled his way towards us. As he came closer, I noticed his baggy trousers were held up by a piece of string tied around his skinny waist. His hair was long, blond and unkempt. His small, once elegant boots lacked laces and polish. He was dressed in an old open jacket and shirt that only had two buttons.

He was probably two years younger than me. His nose was runny and he looked hungry and sad as he stood aside and watched us. Father finished his lunch, so he stood up, reached into his pocket and took out an apple. He held the apple out for the boy who grabbed it and gobbled it – core, grub, and all. When he got to the core, I thought he would throw it away because of a grub in it, but he quickly stuffed the last morsel in his mouth. There was a hint of a smile on his dirty face.

I waved to him as we went around the corner and he watched as we drove away. I didn't think much more about him except that each time I bit into an apple with a grub in it, I would remember the poor little boy who was too hungry to even mind the grub.

During the school holidays, Father often took Pete and David with him to fell trees for a local timber mill. Once fallen, the bark was stripped off the whole log and then cut into lengths suitable for milling. The bush they worked was over the creek and was owned by Mr Cowden. It was a mile and a half walk there. One day, they came home and told us they found a big gum tree. With their axes, they cut a scarf into the trunk so that it would fall between two other trees. They left the tree to come home and milk the cows.

Next morning, they were up early to milk before going to finish cutting the tree with the long two-man saw.

We helped Mother take a picnic lunch over to the working men. We got there not long before the giant fell. While we stood some distance away, Pete and David made the final strokes, back and forth with the saw. A steel wedge was driven in the gap the saw made some time before. Father picked up the sledgehammer and gave the wedge another couple of lusty blows which were followed by a series of loud cracking sounds. With a whoosh the tree crashed to the ground. Then silence. The little birds that were flitting around singing as they went, suddenly stopped. Even the wind seemed to be silent. It was as if God was saying, 'I want a moment's silence to remember this creation of mine.' It was, after all, a magnificent gum tree.

There was a special place in the bush I liked to go when I wanted to be alone. It was about five hundred yards from the farm house. A white gum tree stood beside a small running stream and on the other side of the bank was a beautiful patch of wild violets and maidenhair fern, all growing through short green moss. The beauty of the flowers and the memory of that spot, still come back to me at times when I have been wanting to get away from some of the crowded, bustling places I found myself in. I tried very hard to remember a poem by Jane Taylor that we were taught at school. Only a few lines of 'The Modest Violet' came to me then: 'Down in a green and shady bed, a modest violet grew, its stalk was bent, it hung its head, as if to hide from view.' The last verse inspired me most. 'Then let me to this valley go this pretty flower to see, that I may also learn to grow in sweet humility.'

When Father bought our Auban ute, we went to a little church in Rokeby, ten miles away to the south. This church comprised mostly one family of Ronalds with two other families as well as three single adults. We spent four happy years there. Oscar Ronalds had three sons – two married with children about our ages. On Sundays after church, we often went to Oscar Ronald's home for lunch. They possessed a lovely home with all stunning furniture and crockery such as I had never seen before. I always enjoyed those visits. Oscar grew daffodils and he propagated new varieties. Sometimes we went to one of his other sons' homes. Harold's family of six children lived over the road opposite to the family homestead. Eric, the younger son's family, consisted of four boys and he built his home about a quarter of a mile over the paddock from where Oscar lived.

In our church there was a family called the Dawsons. When I first got to know them they seemed strange, because I didn't know a son who was so much like his father – tall and thin – while their daughter was like her short, stocky mother. Jack was ten years old and Joan was about two years younger. There were six long wooden pews down each side of the small church. The Dawson family usually sat in the third row back from the front. Malcolm and I sat in the front seat with our parents. The older boys in our family sat in the back row with some of the older boys from the Ronald's families. Together the boys filled up the pews each side of the aisle. When service ended the children escaped from their parents to join the other young people outside while the adults lingered to catch up with their friends inside the building.

Mother called us when it was time to leave church. That Sunday, while waiting in our car for Father to come, I watched the Dawson family all get into their clean modern car. Jack sat next to his dad. With some difficulty his mum got in behind him. Joan sat at the back beside her mum. It was a hot day, so I opened the window to let some cool breeze in. Mrs Dawson did the same and her open window was only about five feet away from where I sat. Mr Dawson started his car and was moving slowly backwards when I poked my head out the open window and shouted, 'Good-bye Mrs Fatty Arbuckle.' As soon as I said those words, I knew they couldn't be taken back. Mr Dawson drove off.

Mother, who was sitting behind me was appalled. She said, 'John, you and I are going to see Mrs Dawson next Sunday and you are going to apologise to her.'

To a boy of six, that was punishment supreme. I wouldn't have been so sorry for myself if Father had heard me and used the strap on me. Then it would have been all over with and I could sleep that night. Instead, my dilemma plagued me at home, at school and at play. What would I say to Mrs Dawson? I was often in this situation before but only to apologise to my brothers. I endured a full week of misery until I went up to Mrs Dawson and said I was sorry for having spoken like I did.

She smiled and said, 'Always try and be kind to people who don't look the same as you.'

That was a great lesson for me to learn. Seventy years have gone by since Mother and Mrs Dawson both taught me to always respect others and not say unkind things to anyone. I mostly have accepted their good advice.

We moved to Drouin West in April 1948. The new farm was eighteen miles from Neerim South which enabled us to go to the same church at Rokeby. This farm was much less isolated than the one we lived in at Neerim South. There was a beautiful row of trees leading to our farmhouse. They were oak and other deciduous trees which in autumn made a riot of beautiful yellow, red and gold colour.

Ours was a large, rundown house which took ages to tidy up. Each of the four spacious bedrooms was graced with their own fireplace, but the lounge had a different fireplace with beautiful wooden panels set off by curved pieces of wood at each end of the mantelpiece surrounding the fireplace. During the cleaning of the house, Mother found an old half-sovereign gold coin behind one of the mantelpieces. This became one of the treasures she kept to pass on in the family.

A corridor ran the length of the house and the doors for each room opened onto it. The back door was on the southern side with a porch over it, while the west and north sides featured a wrap-around veranda which gave the house a colonial look. The kitchen was close to the back door and was twenty steps on a concrete path to the garden gate. When it rained, we didn't use the back-garden gate because the cows came past it for milking and with their big hooves turned the area into a mud bog.

The milking shed was about seventy-five yards away. I remember getting stuck in the mud and having to pull my feet out of both boots, leaving my socks inside them. I rolled up my trousers and squelched my way across ten paces of thick, stinking mud. While I washed the mud off my feet and legs, I wondered how to retrieve my gumboots. Fortunately, there was a heap of wooden fence palings under a tree nearby and I used four of the palings as stepping stones. I laid one across the mud and with the other one I wobbled before putting it into place. I could now reach the buried gumboots, so I pulled them out of the mud. Two of my brothers came by and laughed at my plight. They gave some ineffective advice and didn't offer to help me as they sauntered away. My hands, feet and legs were covered in the gooey, stinking mud. I was flustered, embarrassed and mad at myself. Still, I laboured on by carrying the boots to safety and returning with a spade from the garden to dig out the two palings. My feet and legs by this time were freezing cold. I washed them again with cold water from the tank. Mother's face was like dark storm clouds when she saw my filthy clothes.

The school at Drouin West was different from the one at Neerim

South. We only needed to walk a mile and a half to school, across the farm, over the boundary fence, through a small patch of bush to the main road. There, we turned right, and it was about a mile along the side of the tar-sealed road to the school gate. There were fewer pupils, a smaller play-area and it was more organised. The teaching staff was made up of two ladies and Mr Millar, the Headmaster. Mr Millar gave David a hard time by hitting him over the ears with his hands or twisting his ears if he couldn't do his work. David had trouble with his ears, so our parents complained to the teacher and he stopped the punishment. However, this didn't stop the fluid coming out of David's ears, so our parents took David to an ear specialist in Melbourne, who gave a homeopathic remedy that cleared up the infection.

We often saw a red, double-cab Bedford truck being driven along the road while we were going to and from school. Both sides of the doors had been painted with big black letters, PMG and underneath in small print was, Post Master General's Department. All the children at school knew and used the nickname for PMG as 'Pig's Meat and Gravy'. The PMG department was responsible for the maintenance of all the telephone lines throughout Victoria. These were round posts placed in the ground in a row along the side of the road, with a gap of about twenty yards between each post. There were three wooden cross members starting at the top with the shortest one that held ten porcelain insulators, the next one down, about fifteen inches, held twelve insulators and the third cross member held fourteen insulators. The cross members were all bolted to the posts and it made them look like a row of bare Christmas trees standing along the side of the road. The insulators purpose was for keeping the telephone wires in place and making sure the same wires didn't touch anything else around them. They were four inches round in the widest part which sloped down from the top and they looked much like small capped umbrellas. The telephone wires were tied on separately with a short piece of wire in a groove, just underneath the wide part of each insulator.

On the way home from school, our family and another family of boys broke dozens of these telephone insulating cups on the telegraph poles. We threw stones and hit the edge of the insulator on the widest part to cause it to break. It was also part of the game to get the stone between all the other wires. The older boys were keeping a tally of their strikes to see who would get the most. However, we realised that not only was the 'Pigs' Meat and Gravy' unhappy with us, but our parents were very cross because they were visited by the PMG informing them of what we did. When we got home from school that afternoon, we were questioned about this vandalism. I only broke a couple of insulators as my problem was getting the stones that far. Malcolm had only just started school and his throwing arm was not developed enough or he would have shared in the punishment. We confessed and were all given a hiding with the slipper. Pete as eldest got the most and David about the same, Jim got a little less, Graeme still less, and I suffered least of all. I could hear the others bawling in their rooms when the punishment was dished out. In fact, we started making a noise as soon as the first stroke was made hoping that the more noise we made, the less severe the punishment. We deserved all the hidings we got, especially that one. It must have cost a lot of money to fix what we damaged, but at the time I thought it was another game, but somehow, I knew it was wrong.

Father bought the old Packard four-seater bus soon after we arrived at Drouin West. It was a long, rectangular vehicle and the front left passenger door wouldn't open because the lock was broken. Mother usually sat in one of the back seats. The very back seat was comfortable, with an armrest in the middle and lots of legroom. While sitting there, it was impossible to hear the conversation from the two front seats.

One Sunday morning we went to church at Rokeby, then home for a quick lunch before going to collect other children for Sunday School. There was a steep, downhill, winding bush road which we had to negotiate over a river bridge. The Packard was in low gear while backfiring as the motor fought not to run faster than the gears would allow. Graeme and I were in the front seat beside Father and smelt the smoke. Then we saw the flames through the cracks in the floor. Father struggled to bring the bus to a halt at the bottom of the hill as the flames were getting quite high by now. We stopped suddenly beside a pile of damp sand. Graeme and I scrambled out the open window. We got such a fright we were both out even before anyone else escaped from the burning bus. There was no time to lose. We were told to throw sand on the flames to put out the fire. The flames were soon put out and all the wiring of the engine was charred. We missed Sunday School that day, and for a week or two after, while the old Packard was being fixed. Father was alone in the front seat until he eventually got the door fixed.

Four months after our arrival at Drouin West there was some talk of Father looking for another job. Mother told me to be quiet about it and the reason given was that the farm owner made several verbal promises that he couldn't keep. A friend at church told Father about a farm at Willung and he took Father and Mother to meet the owner and to have a look over the farm. They liked what they saw, though I knew nothing of their decision till a month before we left Drouin West. I was very happy.

Sunday School meant a lot to me. We learnt choruses and memory verses from the Bible. It was as if God spoke to me whenever we sang the song, although at the time, I didn't realise how significant it would be for me. 'Two little eyes to look to God, two little ears to hear His word, two little feet to walk in His way, two little lips to sing His praise, two little hands to do His will and one little heart to love Him still.'

Was God telling me to give myself to Him? A man was speaking to us about the love Jesus was offering 'me' and how He died on the cross just for me. I couldn't get over Jesus loving me enough to die for me. I began to weep, and the tears didn't stop for some time. Then we all sang this chorus. 'Into my heart, into my heart, come into my heart Lord Jesus, come in today, come in to stay, come into my heart Lord Jesus.'

In a simple child-like way, I asked the Lord Jesus to come into my heart and forgive my sin. From that time, I believe He has always been with me. However, I was still learning. I often failed Him when I did or said something wrong. Sometimes I would feel that the Lord Jesus left me, but it was I who left Him. The words, 'Into my heart, come into my heart Lord Jesus,' always remind me of the great love Jesus has for me, and my commitment to show my love to Him.

It was soon after this that we moved seventy miles further east to Willung, towards the end of 1948.

CHAPTER 2

When we moved to the Willung farm, it had seventy head of cattle and fifty pigs. Of the seventy, there were forty-five milking cows, a bull in his own fenced paddock, some calves that were recently weaned, and some young heifers. Milking the cows and feeding the pigs was a twice-daily chore. The cows took a couple of hours to milk and the pigs half an hour to feed. The old draughty cowshed with its muddy yard outside, didn't have concrete. Inside, the shed had a brick floor. About twenty cows could get into the shed at a time, eight of them in the wooden bales. The shed was built so that each cow could have a feed from a box while she was being milked. One boy was given the job of putting some bran or oats into their feeding box each time another cow entered the bale. This supplementary feed was only given when grass was in short supply. It helped with the milk production.

If I was feeding the pigs, I washed out the feeding trough with a broom and water. Then I gave them a measured amount of grain and enough milk to fill their empty stomachs. At first they squealed and scrambled around for their food, but after about ten minutes of gulping away they all quietened down for a sleep. Before drifting off, it seemed to me as though they were saying thank you with each individual grunt of contentment. Pigs have their own personalities too. There was almost always a small runt in most litters. He or she was the one who always got the least food and grew the slowest. All pigs love food of whatever kind. They are not at all fussy. Thick sour milk full of blowfly maggots all went down with great relish and delight.

Once the rabbit-proof fence was erected around the house, a large area was dug over for a garden and this slowly came into production. Pig and cow manure were left to rot down for fertiliser, and because the soil was light and sandy, these elements helped our plants thrive.

There were three gates to the garden, and the two on the back fence were fitted with weight and pulley arrangements so they would shut themselves. This piece of Father's genius stopped the cattle from getting into the garden. However, on a couple of occasions when the cows got in, it was a sad day especially for Mother, who put a lot of work into the flower garden. One day, a gate was left open and a sow ran into the garden with her litter of ten piglets. The havoc they wrecked before we got them out left Mother in tears.

Some moonlight nights two or three of us would spend an hour or two after dinner turning over the grey damp soil. At these times there were little glow-worms in the soil that gave off their iridescent light when exposed. Our parents made sure that the potatoes, turnips, carrots and parsnips were rotated and not set in the same place every year. The new potatoes and the peas were usually ready for Christmas. Mother used to boil or bake white onions and serve one on each of our dinner plates with other meat and veggies. They were delicious.

In the summer it was quite a problem to keep the garden properly watered. However, it was a source of lovely fresh vegetables and hours of pleasure for Mother as she managed the flower garden. She planted some lovely crops of dahlias, delphiniums, chrysanthemums, poppies, gladioli and roses. Not all us six boys took an interest in this part of the farm, but we all were expected, at different times, to do some work in it. As young kids we tried to outdo each other with the biggest vegetables in our own patch. This was not all a success. However, I did enjoy helping both Mother and Father in the different areas of the garden and having a go on my own.

A path led on an angle from a gate at the corner of the back fence, to a gate in the centre of the front fence by the pink climbing rose. Father put up some posts and wires to grow three boysenberry plants a yard from the edge of the path. Once established, these vines were a break between Mother's flower garden and the vegetable patch, but more importantly, they produced billies of summer fruit. I used to help pick them and my motto was one for the billy and one for my mouth, at least until I had eaten more than enough. The juice used to spill out if I put too many in my mouth at once, but it was a wonderful sensation to have a gob full of juicy, dark-red berries and then let them slide into the dark recesses of my stomach. Ah, that lovely sweet taste of berries picked fresh from the vine. Mother knew that we ate more than our share because there were tell-tale signs around our lips, but she laughed at us when we came inside and gave her our billies full of fresh berries. Some Mother made into jam, while others she preserved in jars to have when fresh fruit was unavailable.

When I was nine, a seedling peach tree grew behind the toilet without even being watered or being cared for. I was keeping my eyes on its first crop of six peaches to see when they ripened. A little squeeze on each of the six went on for a few days until I discovered that two of them changed colour and were softening. I left them two more days and when no one was looking, I went to give them another squeeze. This time the first two were ripe. I picked the first peach and hid behind the tree where the juicy fruit was quickly consumed. Dropping the peach stone, I stamped the evidence into the ground and wiped my sticky hands down my overalls. I noticed that all the others had changed colour, less than the one I knew was ripe. I should walk away, but I couldn't resist. I reached out and picked another ripe peach, but then decided to pick them all. I did, until my pockets were bulging with five nice peaches. 'I know what I'll do', I said to myself, 'I'll go a little way over the brow of the hill, sit among the bracken so as not to be seen and have a secret feast of peaches'. And that's what I did. Well, the first of the five was delicious. The second one I tried was somewhat hard and sour, but it was too good to waste so the stone was all I threw away. There were only three of my feed left. I took the next softest and on the third bite I needed to stop chewing because I got the niggle in my stomach of the feeling one gets when one eats too much unripened fruit. I threw the evidence over the hill into the tussocks and the other two peaches went the same way with only one bite from each. I sauntered back up the hill, climbed over the fence, past the wood pile to the back gate as though nothing had happened. Mother was eagerly awaiting the ripening of those peaches and at dinner that night asked if anyone knew what happened to them. No one owned up. The lamp light must have been dim or they would have seen my blushing face.

When I was older, I reminded Mother of the incident and she said she couldn't remember, yet my sin pricked my conscience. It wasn't until I told Mother what I did that I knew complete freedom from my guilt. God forgave me, but I was learning that if I offended someone, I was to put it right with them too. Mother didn't remember the incident. That is just like God, who doesn't remember my sin anymore when I confess it to Him. Freedom at last.

At least two years we were at Willung, the paddock of hay was destroyed by a plague of caterpillars. They could eat the goodness out of the paddock in a couple of days. One year the ground was thick with these little black creatures vying for anything they could eat. They got caught in still water and the smell of hundreds of them rotting was putrid. They ate the grass and the garden vegetables and after a couple of weeks, they were all gone. I often wondered where they all went.

The most effective method to rid pasture of bracken was to cut it off. This was done two or three times a year for eight to ten years before complete eradication became possible. On the flat land, the horse and hay mower were used, and this would take four or five days to complete. On the slopes and close to trees and fences, it all was done by hand. For this purpose, either a two-sided flat blade on a handle or a curved sickle-like blade was used. The blades were sharpened either with a stone or file. Cutting ferns was hard work and it would take several weeks of Saturdays or school holidays to complete the job. Once a year, Alex Ronalds paid us an hourly rate to cut the ferns, so we were able to earn pocket money for this job. They always seemed to get cut quicker when there was payment involved.

Grubbing out tussocks was another farm problem that required continual work. However, these were not as difficult to eradicate as the ferns. They were dug out using a hoe. We called this hoe a grubber, as it was somewhat stronger than a normal garden hoe. A swampy tussock's sharp flat leaves could inflict cuts unless care was exercised. The ones that grew with a round smooth leaf were in drier areas of the farm. Alex Ronalds brought his John Deere tractor to plough the swampy areas in the summertime. The land soon came back into production. Occasionally the tractor got bogged in the mud, and then the horse came and pulled it out.

This tractor engine was started on petrol till it had warmed up. A tap was turned which allowed a type of kerosene used in airplane engines of the day to flow into the motor. To start it there was a fly wheel on one side of the motor that was turned to start the motor. One day, just as Alex Ronalds drove away after a day's work on the machine, I turned the fly wheel and the tractor engine burst into life. I didn't have a clue how to stop it. David came out of the house – laughing and put an end to my embarrassment because he knew what to do.

Several drains crossed the farm taking off surplus water to the creek. One had a permanent spring which issued a clear water flow all the year round. The drains needed to be kept free of weed and tussocks, so this was another twice-a-year job. For cleaning drains, a blade on a handle was used to cut the weed on the sides, and a fork with bent tines was used to haul the weed out of the drain. If the drain was badly in need of a clean, fifty yards a day was good going for one person. This was a dirty job as we would get splashed with mud and dirty water. There were lots of interesting things to find in these drains. Small eels and fish, millions of frog eggs, tad-poles, and frogs together with water snails and leeches. There were dragonflies of all colours, shapes and sizes and black beetles that jerked across the top of the water. There was even a platypus.

One day, when Pete was slashing down the side of a drain, he hit and killed a small platypus which was hiding under the weeds. It was about a foot long. As platypuses were protected and not to be killed, Father phoned the policeman and told him the story. The next day, we took the animal to school for a nature lesson. We were able to closely see the duck-like bill, the sharp claws on its webbed feet, feel the thick soft fur on the body and flat broad tail. The plat-ypus is a most unusual animal which digs a burrow for a nest where the female lays her eggs, and they hatch a few days after. On rare occasions, we saw platypuses in the creek. There were two spots I knew where they lived, but I had to be very quiet to see these shy creatures. I often wondered where they went when the creek flooded. I read in my Bible that God knows when a sparrow falls to the ground. I believed He watched and knew every detail of all the animals, fish, plants and insects in all the world. My heavenly Father sure cares for me too.

There were two old things I particularly loved at Willung. They were the old Packard and the old horse Bobbin. I loved them because they both were comfortable to be around and I wasn't scared of either. Bobbin was like a friend I could go and talk to. I rode him while hanging onto his mane or watched him at work and admired his strength.

The old Packard had a different kind of attraction. Malcolm and I spent many hours of play in the old bus, pretending to be someone important, who sat in the special plush back seat while the other was driving. The driver made the engine sound of the gear changes, and when stopping, the noise of squealing brakes. The seat was too low to see over the steering wheel so when I was the driver, I knelt on the seat so I could do my job properly. Malcolm and I admired the walnut trim around the dashboard and the smoothness of sections of the steering wheel that had the same kind of walnut timber between the spokes. The smell of old oil lingered in the front seat, but by the time I got to the fourth seat back, the only aroma was the musty smell of the carpet, which I was quite used to. The brief years of delightful childhood play were being left behind for Malcolm and me. The old Packard was sold to two men who were building a new bridge over the creek. They used it as a caravan, and it saved them going twenty-five miles to their homes each night.

Sometime after we moved to Willung, one of my brothers learned of an old orchard somewhere up on the top of one of the ridges. It wasn't long before we set off to see what we could find. At first, we followed familiar paths but soon we were in new territory. There was an overgrown kind of track we took up the hill and at the top it turned sharp right. We were an hour or so from home and some of the party were cautious about going on. But the goal was not reached so the call to finish the course prevailed. There were more doubts as the distance from home grew considerably. We came at last to a clear space thick with bracken and still there was no sign of an orchard. Again, the doubting questions came as we sweated on. More bush was in front of us. As we came over the brow of the hill there was another clearing and some fruit trees. Rabbits tore off in all directions. We crossed over a worn track leading down hill to the left and to the right, although we hardly noticed this track in our haste to get some of the fruit. There was a crumbling brick chimney, a dilapidated shed near some encroaching tea-tree. We found a couple of deep, dry holes where wells were dug. Apricots, plums and two mulberry trees had long since seen their best years. Some plums and apricots were ripe enough to eat. We took some home to prove we found the orchard. It was about three miles each way and all through bush. Having these kinds of sorties helped us have a good sense of direction in strange places. These were great times.

For the next five years, we went to the orchard about the time we thought the fruit would be ripe. Slowly however, the trees were more and more diseased with moss and dead wood. Someone chose this spot for a settlement, built a house, cleared some land and worked to grow the trees whose fruit we enjoyed. There was no permanent water for miles. A few struggling fruit trees and crumbling bricks where the chimney had once been were all that remained of the battler's hard work. Was it a bush fire, drought, ill health, no water, poverty or even death that had driven the landowner to quit? We would never know.

We lived at Willung for two and a half years before Father decided to take at least thirty cows to a paddock he hired for two months over winter. The plan was to use the same tracks we took to the old orchard. From there follow the downhill track – north – that lead about two miles to the paddock were the cows would go. Pete and

David had previously explored the tracks on their bikes. Most of the track grew shorter bracken in the centre and were used occasionally by four-wheel drive vehicles. These tracks were ideal for taking our cows on, though they were rough in places where erosion caused washouts. The track came out of the bush at the bottom of the hill about a mile and a half from the old orchard. The paddock the cows would be put in was half a mile further on a straight road with a wide verge.

It was a cool, blustery Saturday morning when three of my older brothers and I, headed off with the cows. I was delegated to stop the cows going on the sandy track towards the main road while Jim was sent in the opposite direction to move the cows up the hill instead of straight ahead. The cows quickly settled into the routine. At the top of the hill, David went ahead to send the cows in the right direction. It was important that all the cows were kept reasonably close together, so we wouldn't miss any in the bush. When they did stray from the track, Pete or David ran and brought them back. This was all new territory for the cows. There were a couple of older cows who seemed to lead the others and keep up a steady pace for them to follow. When we turned and started down the hill, they went a little faster. By this time, the cows kept together so it made it much easier and quicker as we got closer to our destination. Father was waiting with the gate opened to the paddock where the cows were going. He was very pleased to see us, especially after he counted all the cows. They would have a 'holiday' here for eight weeks before we repeated the task in the opposite direction. Shifting the cows like this, became a regular adventure to be undertaken for each of the years we remained living at Willung.

For my eighth birthday I was given a small King James Bible and in spite of all the 'thees' and 'thous', this kind of English was not strange to us because it was the Bible language used back then.

I treasured my own new Bible and I took comfort from Genesis which said, 'God made all sorts of wild animals, livestock, and small animals, each able to produce offspring of the same kind.' I thought, God has prepared his special way of making this happen with all the living creatures, plants, animals, fish, birds and us humans, able to reproduce. However, when I thought of all of man's creations including the Packard, I couldn't think of any that could reproduce themselves. I was not surprised that God could say, 'That is very good,' for all His wonderful creations.

Once Graeme and I were sent down the farm to catch Bobbin. After we caught him, I led him beside the post which Graeme was standing on. I passed the reigns to Graeme and soon he was on Bobbin's bare back. I got onto Bobbin the same way. We started to walk Bobbin towards the shed to get him harnessed for work, but he started to jog along, and we got the giggles. Graeme in front could hold onto the reins and steer, whereas I held onto Graeme. The giggling soon developed into laughter and because of the jogging gait, we both abandoned hanging on for laughter and fell off. It was at least four and a half feet to the ground, and the laughter turned to tears, especially as the old horse jogged away and we had to catch him again.

Harvesting time was always lots of fun for me. Usually, three neighbours came to lend a hand. The men talked about horses and how helpful and faithful horses were. All the while the men were getting to know each other. They shared these times around stops for food and drinks that were usually prepared by the wife of the farmer whose farm was being worked on.

We used to take the food and drinks down to the workers from Mother's kitchen and we would hear the stories that were exchanged.

In the spring of each year, a paddock was closed off from the cows, to allow the grass and clover to grow about eighteen inches high ready for cutting. Mr Hair, Mr Farrah and Mr Taylor came to our farm for two days to assist us the same as Father, Pete and David helped them. Father had to co-ordinate the days when the hay was dry enough to make a haystack. Mother prepared food and drink for us all. Mr Taylor was a leader in the community, a kind man with four children. He drove a canvas top Chev car which seemed to me to be as old as our Packard. He was soon to be distinguished by his new dark blue Holden – the first in the district.

Bobbin was harnessed to the mower early in the morning and Father sat on the metal seat, between the two iron wheels, while he steered Bobbin into the paddock. He stopped Bobbin, got off the mower and let the heavy steel blade holder down onto the long grass. Father carefully oiled all the moving parts on the mower before he and Bobbin were ready to go. When Father was back in the seat, he took hold of the reins, gave them a quick flip at the same time as he shouted at Bobbin, 'Get up!' They moved off with the mower making a distinguished zick-zick, zick-zick sound as it left a swath of mown grass behind. Next time around, Father made sure the right-hand wheel of the mower was in the gap that was mowed so the grass to be cut wouldn't be trampled by Bobbin or the mower. It was a frustrating job as often the mower would clog if the grass was too damp or thick. The V-shaped blades needed sharpening, and sometimes the poor old horse needed a spell from this heavy work in the hot sun. This job took the whole day to complete.

When the cut grass was dry enough, Father phoned Mr Taylor who had previously arranged to bring his horse to use him as well as Bobbin. Mr Taylor arrived with his horse at about the same time Mr Hair and Mr Farrah came by car to help build the haystack.

Father drove Bobbin to pull the rake, but when the other men arrived, he left Pete in charge of the raking. The rake had two five-foot high steel wheels, a steel seat halfway between the wheels, and under the seat twenty curved steel tines with a point on the end that ran along the top of the ground. There was a dumping mechanism, which allowed Pete to steer the horse back and forth across the field and catch enough dry hay to fill the rake, and then deposit it in three-foot-high rows.

Mr Taylor's horse was harnessed to a sweep with no seat. Mr Taylor held two handles that were attached to the back of the frame and walked as the horse went forward. The horse was attached by two very long trace chains on the outer sides of the sweep. There were sixteen three-foot long wooden, metal tipped spikes sticking out in front of the frame. These spikes were six inches apart and attached to the frame. They were dragged along the ground and the horse was steered along a row of raked hay until the sweep was full. This was then taken to the place where the stack was being built and upended while the horse pulled the empty sweep away ready for the next load. This loose hay was then forked up onto the stack with a pitchfork. This was a three-pronged long handle fork especially used for pitching hay. There were usually two or three people building the stack layer by layer, making sure it was well trampled down. The top of the stack was finished so the rain would run off and most farmers covered their stacks. There was no plastic sheeting, so Father got us to help sew hessian sacks together to form a rug for the stack. Some stacks were round and others square or rectangle. There was a real art in making a good haystack.

Before we left Willung, a hay baler was brought to our hay paddock and compressed the loose hay into rectangular bales about eighteen-inches wide and deep, and three-feet long. As the hay moved through the machine the bale was tied up with two pieces of thin wire that held the hay together. This meant that the haystacks were no longer nice round shape, but the countryside was littered with square or rectangle stacks.

One day when we went to school, Mr Taylor was driving a tractor instead of his horse. The tractor had a mower on the back, and he was cutting the grass. Malcolm and I watched for a while and we rode a little slower. The next afternoon, he was raking the hay with the rake on his tractor. Early in the morning, we noticed a man with a bigger tractor towing what looked like a new baler. Sure enough, on our way home from school the hay bales were scattered throughout the paddock. Mrs Taylor drove the tractor and trailer while her husband walked behind to pick up the next bale. No horse was in sight. He didn't need Bobbin to come and help him that year or ever again.

Bobbin, for most of his thirty-two years, helped each summer in all the operations on several farms in the area. His mane and whiskers were quite grey by this time. He was getting thin because his teeth were worn out. Father contacted the yard that took old animals for pet food. Next Saturday some of us boys were delegated to take him the seven miles by road to the yard. Our new horse, Trixie was harnessed to the cart and Bobbin was tied to the back of the cart by a halter. This is a rope around his face with a lead on it, so a horse can be led along or tied to a fence post.

All went well for the first five miles. We were through the bush and out on the open stretch of straight road. My impatient brothers said we were going too slow. They delegated me to ride Bobbin. I got on Bobbin's back when the cart was stopped, and David unhitched the halter rope from the cart, and gave it up to me. I indicated to Bobbin it was time to go. The old nag turned ninety degrees to the left and headed straight for the fence which was about twenty-five yards from the road. I couldn't steer him. There was no bit in his mouth. The others trotted on ahead hoping that Bobbin would go faster, but no, he just walked slowly along.

There was only one tree on this fence line. It was a low-branched macrocapa. The branches stretched over the fence and we were headed straight for it. Sure, the pace was slow but here was a last chance for this old horse to rub his back on the limb of the tree. I called him to stop. I pulled as hard as I could on the rope in a vain effort to turn his nose. As he ducked his old head to walk sedately under the lowest branch, I was swept over his rump and landed flat on my back among the roots of the tree. I was totally winded, but my old friend Bobbin was waiting for me as I got gingerly to my feet again. My three brothers in the cart, roared their heads off with laughter at my predicament. They at least had the sense to tie Bobbin back to the cart and let him plod at his usual slow pace till we reached his final resting place. Sadly, our old faithful Bobbin was put down. The year was 1953 and horses were making way for tractors. I was somewhat groggy for the homeward journey and have no memory of it, but I suspect we went much faster with David's younger horse Trixie towing the cart, minus Bobbin.

Two years before Bobbin took me for my last ride, Mr Mac, one of the neighbours, stopped Malcolm and me while we were going home from school. I wondered what we did to cause him to speak to us for the first time. We were pleasantly surprised when he asked us if we would like an orphaned lamb to raise for a pet. I was so excited, I thanked him for the offer, but told him that we would have to ask our parents first. They would also need to know how much it would cost. Mr Mac gave us assurance that it wouldn't cost anything.

We raced home without stopping at the usual places. My thoughts were on a lamb for a pet and I wondered if Mother and Father could be persuaded to let me have one. Looking after a lamb was a totally new experience for us. Mother knew it would take a lot more feeding for the first few weeks. She knew that it would be her task to look while I was at school. Mother had a soft heart for any orphaned creature.

When Father agreed that we would give it a try, we went in the

Packard back to the Mac's farm and came home with little Lambie. He was quite small and weak as he was only one day old. By the time we brought him home Mother had a warm box prepared for him to sleep in. I fed him warm cows' milk from a bottle with a teat on it. We soon developed a routine of four feeds in the daytime. At night he was kept in an empty chicken coop. At first light, he would make a great noise until I fed him. He drank the milk from a large lemonade bottle, three times a day and was soon too big to fit in the chicken cage. He was eating grass too which meant we didn't have to feed him so often. But, whenever he did demand some milk, he used to stand by the back gate and 'Baa, Baa' until we gave him what he wanted. When he was small, I would call him and he would come for a cuddle or to hear me chat to him.

Lambie was never any real problem until he got to teenage months. For a sheep that was about nine months old. He wanted to come inside our house where it was forbidden for any animal his size. This time he waited outside the gate until it was opened and then forced his way past the legs of the person opening the gate, dashed up the two steps and went straight through the fly screen door. He continued walking around the kitchen peeing on the floor as he went. When he emptied his bladder, he marched straight out the hole he made as though he was king of the castle. Father fixed the fly screen door and thought that would be the end of the story. However, two weeks later while I was carrying an armful of wood to fill the box at the back door, Lambie forced his way past me at the gate and smashed his way through again. Father and Mother were very cross. Father decided to fix a piece of plywood, so it filled in the bottom half of the door. A few days later I pretended to stop Lambie at the gate to see what he would do. He stopped short two inches away from the plywood. He looked at me with some indignation, as if to say, 'Why have you stopped me having some fun?' I laughed loudly.

After two months, he was completely weaned off milk and was less than half grown. Lambie got along well with all the other animals on the farm, especially the cows. He used to lead them, and the cows willingly followed him. We often saw him leading the cows back to the milking shed in time for milking. I wondered who gave him the sense? If it had been Father, my brothers or me, we would have tried to teach him to 'get in behind' the cows. He led from the front with such grace and elegance without any reward or even a thank you.

There was at least one other lesson I was keen to set my heart at rest about. It happened when Lambie was a little over two years old. Father took a phone call from Mr Mac who was shearing his sheep and he offered to shear Lambie too. Father accepted Mr Mac's offer with gratitude. By this time Lambie was fully grown, so I led him into the spacious area at the back seat of the Packard. I sat on the seat while he stood quite still except to adjust his feet as we went around corners on the way to the Mac's place. With Lambie at my side, I followed Father and Mr Mac as they went up a wooden ramp into the shearing shed.

Mr Mac was a kind but very shy man who was not yet married. He lived with his younger sister and elderly parents in their large family home. His garb was a white sweat-stained singlet, old brown trousers and a pair of brown soft boots. Red hair on his arms and chest was the same colour as his whiskers. Long wispy strands of red hair, from a partly balding head, reached to the singlet at the back of his neck. It was noisy, with the motor going for the shearing plant and the constant bleating of the sheep waiting to be sheared. Three other men were busy shearing sheep when I led Lambie up the wooden ramp near the place where the sheep were shorn.

While Mr Mac went into the place alongside the other shearers, I took Lambie over to him, spoke to Lambie while I untied his lead and told him to be a good boy while he was getting his wool cut off.

I watched and listened as Mr Mac took Lambie. He bent over him, held a front leg in each hand, and before Lambie knew where he was, Mr Mac tipped Lambie onto his back with his hind legs dangling in the air. Lambie was held up so his head was between Mr Mac's knees. With one hand he took the shears and while he held Lambie with the other hand, he gently cut all the wool off. He started by going first around Lambie's neck, front and back leg and down the other side in the same pattern. He finished with all the wool spread out like a rug the same shape of Lambie if he had been flattened out. Lambie stood shaking for a few moments while I put his lead on him. He had just lost a coat of four inches of warm wool. He looked a whiter colour and much thinner, but a few days later it all started to grow back again.

I was really wanting to prove God's Word to be true. In our church someone often read from the Bible in Isaiah 53:7,

He [Jesus] was led like a lamb to the slaughter. And as a sheep is silent before the shearers, He did not open his mouth.

These words were written by Isaiah the prophet five hundred years before Jesus was born in Bethlehem. When Jesus did eventually face the cruelty and mock trial before the High Priest and Herod – the Jewish King, Jesus was silent. Lambie was another example to me of the accuracy of the Bible. He proved it to me by not uttering a sound while being shorn.

We thanked Mr Mac for all his kindness, but he still had more to give. He gave Father the address to send Lambie's sugar bag full of eleven-and-a-half-pound fleece of purebred Dorset Short Horn fine wool. I waved goodbye to a smiling Mr Mac as we departed. Eventually, I received a cheque by mail for five pounds for Lambie's wool. I never had so much money in my life. I carried a smile of gratitude for a few days after that and whenever one of my brothers teased me about being a rich sheep farmer. Wool, at that time, was worth good money and the wool from Lambie sold for one hundred and six pence a pound.

Willung was not the usual place to get snow, but one year we did. It was July or August and this cold snap of weather descended bringing with it about three inches of snow. It was quite special for us boys not used to snow. We went out with gloves and coats and played snow fights. We built two snowmen and they lasted a couple of weeks before finally melting away. I remember all the ground covered with the fresh fallen snow, sparkling when the sun peeked through the clouds. It was so cold on our fingers and toes, yet we had great fun. The snow on the ground lingered less than the snowmen. It was melted in two days.

About this time, we saw a Christian movie which showed the snowflakes under a microscope. I was amazed to see that every snowflake had its own unique, intricate pattern. To me they were a square blob of snow falling from the clouds to make larger blocks of snow and ice. But God saw them differently. I wondered what He thought when He knew that I marvelled at His wonderful and beautiful creation.

Our mother had the greatest impact on our family. Father kept strict discipline, but any love and softness in our family came through Mother. She was a great letter writer when time permitted. Her letters were always in a clear hand writing, newsy and informative. She loved good books and music and told us stories of going to concerts in Devonport as a young person. On a cold winter's night, she sometimes sat by the fire and did fine needle work. One great pleasure she had was getting out the good bone china cups or dinner set when we had visitors. Her pet hate was sewing, hence she made few of her own clothes, but she darned all our woollen socks when they got holes in them. This was often, as nylon or synthetic fabrics were not around then. There must have been mountains of ironing, mending and darning that she did over the years. Shirt collars and cuffs were starched when used to go to church or special occasions. Mother always had long hair. It was never cut and, until she died it was tied in a bun at the back of her head. Cut hair to her was against God's command. She was very strong on Biblical principles.

At heart, Mother was a big softie. We could get around Mother and get her to let us do things Father would have said no to. It was at her knees, we learned God's love for us. In the winter she would read serial stories to us as we gathered around the fire and she encouraged us to read for ourselves. She helped us in choosing character-building books. We played board games like Chinese checkers, snakes and ladders, draughts etc, but no card games were allowed as they were considered evil. There were special Bible games for Sunday nights.

There was a difference between Mother's and Father's discipline, though they were of one mind at least in front of us. Obedience was insisted on and we were only given one chance if we were told to do something. This stemmed in part from our Father army stint and from our parents own strict upbringing. Looking back, I can see one good spin off from this and the rest of our days of youth. None of us ever had difficulty taking directions from or working under other people. I suppose each of us could say that at times we felt the punishment rather harsh or unjust, but in most cases, we deserved what we got. We would be strapped only on the backside. However, we all knew the rules and if broken we expected to be punished. What boy didn't try to stretch the rules as far as possible?

For us younger ones, our older brothers were not afraid to give us a punch if they thought we stepped out of line. There was a lot of competition among us and dares, to see who was game to tackle certain things. Play wrestling between us to see who was the strongest, was quite common. There were the occasional fights because of anger, and tears would flow, or a parent stopped the fight if they thought it appropriate. In all this, I have no memory of any of us ever being seriously hurt in any fights. An occasional bruise was all that any of us ever sustained with no black eyes or broken limbs.

We were encouraged by Mother especially, to do well at school with our reading. She taught us good diction and sentence construction and always corrected us. Along with this, was respect for adults and older people. We were told to be polite to everyone and address them with the proper title. We were not permitted to answer our parents back or be cheeky or rude to them. Swearing was not permitted and the threat for breaking this rule was to have our mouth washed out with soap and water. I know the threat was carried out as one of my brothers endured it. Somehow, I managed to survive. Many words used in common language today were considered swear words by Mother. The Lord's name used incorrectly was of course totally forbidden, and we were meant to show respect for people in authority and the royal family.

One of the greatest things our Father taught us was to respect women. He was very severe on any of us who spoke with disrespect to Mother or answered her back. While there were times when heated words were exchanged between them, we were not allowed to speak in anger to them. Our parents argued sometimes for several days. Occasionally a week went by and they wouldn't speak to each other. Even though this happened, there was a deep love and devotion between them. Both possessed very strong characters, and seemingly small decisions like what colour to paint the house, was not solved until some days of either verbal or non-verbal communication, passed between them. As I got older, I realised Mother almost always got her way in these decisions. Did God give us parents so we could learn from their mistakes? If only we learned.

We were not a close-knit family. Each of us six boys have tended to work out our own pattern and way of life. Lessons learned in our early life have sometimes had to be relearned in adulthood. I realised, that mistakes I made in my teenage years, if not corrected, tend to return in a similar form later in life to give me another try at making corrections to my character. The dinner table was the best place for family conversation, but that would depend on the mood of the family or some of the members. Occasionally these times were quite tense, but as a junior member of the party, I usually let that slide past me, unless I was involved.

The cost of keeping six growing boys must have been quite staggering. I remember Pete claiming he ate twelve Weet Bix at one sitting for breakfast, so a packet wouldn't last long at that rate, and six Weet Bix at a time for most of us was not uncommon in our house.

Sunday nights Mother would often play her organ and we would be encouraged to sing hymns especially if there were visitors. This may last an hour or so and we could choose our favourite hymn. On Friday nights there was a church weekly Bible study to which the adults went along with older teenagers. This study was held in the homes and every two months or so it would be at our place. It went from eight o'clock to about nine-thirty. Often, in front of a nice warm fire, many of the farmers nodded off to sleep.

The *Weekly Times* was a farming paper with the latest trends affecting the farming community. There was lots of advertising, and a whole page of comic strips that us boys enjoyed. It was different to a newspaper in that it was smaller in size and stapled, with sixty pages. The daily newspaper which was called *The Age*. The paper, *Weekly Times*, magazines and bread were all delivered with the mail to the box at the start of our sandy track. We had no television, but we did have a radio run off a six-volt car battery. When the battery was flat, we had no radio news or our favourite programmes like the air adventures of Biggles, Dad and Dave, Greenbottle and a programme called D24 which were true stories from the files of the Victorian police.

Our church was nine miles away at Gormandale. At first there were four families who met in a small room of the local hall. The services had no pastor or minister and only the men were able to speak, pray, or give out a hymn. Services usually went an hour and a half, commencing at eleven o'clock. Sometimes there were visiting speakers. Lunch was usually at Alex Ronald's place. Mother and Father ate their lunch inside with Alex and Ivy while us boys took our sandwiches in the car and then played around until we went to Sunday School in a little Union Church. Sunday School classes were by age, much like school. Alex Ronalds was one of my best teachers.

We met in the local hall at the end of each year for a Sunday School anniversary, where tables were loaded with sandwiches, savouries, cream buns and cakes or other delicious things that were good to eat. After all the visitors, parents and children finished eating, the tables were cleared away and the seats put facing the stage for items which were presented by each class. This was followed by the prize giving where awards were given to those who got the top marks in each class for attendance and memory verse learning. Each child was given a book award suitable for their age group. The evening was rounded off with a short message and a prayer of thanks to God.

In our family the Jungle Doctor books were quite popular for a while, but I really liked the coloured comic-style book of the life of Joseph. The drawings of Joseph as a boy, as a youth with his coloured coat, when he was sold into slavery, his imprisonment, his dreams, his promotion and the joy of seeing his father again, made that part of the Bible come alive for me. I read it through many times observing the pictures at the same time as I read the words.

Joseph soon became my favourite character of the Old Testament. I learnt how God tested him in his life in different ways. He came through them all trusting God. While I was learning about Joseph, I was learning about God, His leading of Joseph, God's protection for him and the brilliant result in the end.

In those days I was absorbing something of the greatness and power of my Creator God. The lessons and stories I did take in, proved to be invaluable later in life. Every second week our parents took another short Sunday School at Willung, so after one we would go to the other. It commenced at three o'clock and it was a bit of a rush. Father did most of the teaching using flannelgraphs to illustrate the lessons. Often there was repetition of stories, and us boys could probably have told them from memory, but I have no regrets of learning the truths from the Bible that I needed for daily living as I grew up.

These were limited holidays, but what we had were memorable. On two occasions David and Pete were left at home while the rest of us went for two weeks to a holiday cottage in Lakes Entrance. It was the May school holidays so some of the time was wet, and it was cold, but we had lots of fun. There were fishing expeditions to various places, but the most successful were off the footbridge at night time or from a jetty or two on the harbour. A couple of times we went out to the Tambo River fishing for garfish. It was quite sporting in that we put three hooks on our lines and sometimes caught three fish at once. But these fish were not so nice to eat. At low tide we would go for bait at Lakes Entrance. We were told that live sand-worms were the best bait. These were under the sand and we could only get them at near low tide. A knee-high length of downpipe with a handle at one end for pushing, was used to catch these four-inch-long worms. The hollow end of the downpipe was put over a sand-worm's hole and pushed down. The worm would shoot out his other hole because of the air that was forced into his constricted space. Two of us were usually worked together, one to operate the pump and the other to grab the squiggling worm and put it in the bucket before it escaped back to its hole. These sandworms had legs like a centipede. They were horrible to bait a hook with, especially with cold hands, but sometimes in the excitement of the 'big' catch, anything on the hook was better than nothing.

We took long walks along the beach to the entrance where the fishing boats came into the harbour from the open ocean. We watched them tossing around on high waves as they battled their way over the sand bar to safer waters of the harbour. Our fun times of running down huge sand dunes of clean yellow sand and then puffing and fighting our way back up in the loose sand to repeat the glorious process were very special. There was shell searching along the rugged sea front, and the delicious times when we could choose a favourite ice cream from the local shop. This was something we couldn't do at home because there were no shops nearby.

In 1951 it was the Jubilee year for the state of Victoria. This meant it was fifty years since Victoria became a state of Australia. Special events took place throughout the state to mark the occasion. The Lord Mayor of Melbourne put on a special camp for country children at an army camp. My parents must have heard about it because they sent Graeme and me to the camp. There seemed to be hundreds of kids our age and some older. We went by train and then by bus, arriving quite late at night, very tired from our long journey. We were put to bed in army barracks and there was little sleep that night as everything was so strange for me who felt so lost and alone. However, although there were times of loneliness, I think it was a good experience for learning how to get along with boys from totally different backgrounds to what I knew. The camp was run with strict military discipline, and forever after when

I read war stories those dormitories, parade ground, and eating place were strangely identical in my imagination. We had a medical examination and stood naked while we were passed along a line of doctors, dentists and nurses for various tests. At night time we watched Laurel and Hardy movies and some cowboy ones, things I had never seen before. There was also a time of singing popular songs of the day. This camp was at Portsea which was at the right entrance of Port Phillip Bay. That meant we swam on both the bay beach and the surf beach on the other side of the spit. Once we had a sand castle competition, we played cricket and games on the oval, but the rest is a bit of a blur, except the journey home. The train was a steam engine, and I had my head out the window most of the way. It was good to get back home again.

The next year we went to a Christian camp at Belgrave Heights. This was totally different and most enjoyable with a good Christian content and atmosphere, which I appreciated. Good friends were made at these camps. Pete, who was a leader, introduced us to them. The only bad experience I remember was that I gained a permanent hatred for tenting. It was May school holidays and one wet night I put a finger on the tent above my head. Later I woke, wet and cold with water dripping off the old tent and my bedding all sopping wet. It was miserable for the rest of the windy, sleepless night.

There were three people who, in different ways, really impacted my spiritual life. All three had similar qualities. They were humble, kind, gentle, loving, patient and good men of faith who lived like Jesus would have lived, if he had been on the earth.

I was eight, in 1949, when I first met Ray Atkinson who, with his wife Minnie, stayed at our home for nearly a week. They were on furlough from India where they were missionaries to people who have leprosy. Ray was Mother's second cousin and we didn't meet again after that short visit. He took a real interest in us boys and painted word pictures of what it was like to be a missionary in India, so much so that I wanted to be a missionary when I grew up.

Mr Toby was a different kind of missionary in that he stayed in Australia to work for the Lord. We first met when I was five years old at Neerim South. He lived in and drove a small motor home. He ate his main meal with us at night. In the day time he visited the families in the district. He stayed about a week talking to a lot of people about the Saviour. He gave them a Bible if they showed an interest. Fred Toby was a tall athletic man with a good crop of white hair and a fine-looking gentleman of about sixty years old. He came to our place every year and a little later as I grew bigger, he taught us boys how to play cricket. When he was in his early twenties he was in the NSW cricket team and heard the story of Jesus for the first time. So, he gave up all his ambition for cricket to serve God. Over the years I realised it was like having Jesus unexpectedly calling in on us for a most welcome visit. He was a great man of God.

And then there was Alex Ronalds who – as a farmer – decided to serve the Lord using farming and his daily walk with God. I was seven years old when I first met Alex and he was fifteen years older than me, with a wife and a young son. I didn't know at the time that Alex would become my teacher or coach. I learned so much from him by trying to follow his example. He didn't seek to promote himself, but always put the Lord and others first. He was gracious and humble in everything he did and said. I was greatly blessed to have a friend like Alex whom I could see and talk to. He reminded me of what Jesus would have been like if he was here personally. But, while I looked to all three men, each of them told me to look to the Lord Jesus and keep my eyes fixed on Him. I will always be grateful for the example and care those men showed me. Their exemplary righteous living and faith helped me to grow as a young follower of the Lord.

CHAPTER 3

When our family arrived at Willung, the school population increased from eighteen to twenty-four. New desks were ordered. We took a week off school while the desks came from somewhere else. During the holiday week, Father visited the neighbour east of us and got permission for us to walk across his farm. It was three miles to school by road and only a mile and a half on this shorter route. We crossed our farm to the boundary fence on the eastern side, climbed the fence, walked across the cattle bridge and along his drive to the connecting road. The school was another mile further on. Pete had a bike, so he was home in time to help Father with the milking. David got his bike about a month before the rest of us.

In the meantime, we did have some fun while walking home near the creek. Catching frogs hidden under logs near the bridge and then releasing them back into the water was one of the things we did. But David had a bright idea. He got a hollow straw of dry grass, put the straw up the frog's back-side and blew air into the frog. This immobilised the frog. David looked around and saw some white puff balls of fungi growing nearby. He handed me the bloated frog, picked a puff ball and hollowed out a boat for the frog. Carefully taking the frog from me he put the toad in the white puff ball and bent down and released the frog into the creek. We watched till it floated around the corner and out sight. The next day after school we hurried to get to the spot by the creek where all five of us constructed a boat for our own bloated frog. We released them simultaneously and cheered them on as they gathered speed in the faster flowing water. However, a few yards from the corner mine was caught in an eddy and stopped by the bank. I don't know whose frog won the race, but I often wondered how those poor frogs got rid of a stomach full of boy's bad breath.

One day as I was walking home from school, I saw a snake that swam. I was beside a swampy patch with a pond twenty yards across. My thoughts were somewhere else as I walked towards our boundary fence. In front of me was a brown snake slithering slowly along in the short grass towards the water. I yelled out to David and Jim who were coming behind. As soon as the snake was aware of my presence, he went fast, propelling himself off the foot-high bank to land with a delicate splash in the water of the pond. Then, with very quick movements of his body from side to side, he glided across the water with his head held high. I was amazed at the graceful movement and the speed which this despised creature took to get across the water. David and Jim only got a fleeting glimpse of the serpent as he moved rapidly away in the tussocks on the other side of the pond. I was glad that he escaped.

The four youngest of us subsequently got four brand new bikes. Mine was a blue Healing with a twenty-four-inch wheel size. I thought all my Christmases had come at once. I loved the bike and while learning to ride, I endured many spills. However, the bike was great for getting not only to and from school, but all over the farm and along the bush tracks. Malcolm had a red one the same size as mine. Jim's and Graeme's were twenty-six-inch wheel size and were red and green respectively. Pete and David already rode the biggest bikes with twenty-eight-inch wheels, and of course, all of us were given strict instructions not to ride no hands.

About a year after the bikes were purchased, I had to try this no hands trick. I fell off and got a few cuts and bruises, but this was only the start of the problem. My bike also came off a little worse for wear and Father needed to know the reason for the accident before he fixed it. When he was told he got confessions from some of my other brothers that they showed me this trick. So, we got a choice of punishment. Either we walk to school for a week or we get a thrashing. We chose walking to school. Silly choice. I don't think Malcolm and Pete had tested this form of bike riding, so they experienced a lonely week of getting to and from school. I expect I would have forgotten the incident had we chosen the hiding.

The little country school was on a hill with trees all around the perimeter of the three acres of ground. There was a single class-room, a shelter shed thirty yards from the door and girls' and boys' toilets even further away in other directions. There were tall pine trees and several gums, but no swings or things to play on. There were footy posts and a bare strip for a cricket pitch. The girls were given another gravel place for a basket-ball court beside the top gate. A path from the school door led down the hill to a small gate at the corner of the grounds. Outside this gate our bikes were parked against the fence.

Norm Sinnott was the only teacher. We called him Sir or Mr Sinnott. Norm, when we thought he was out of earshot. He usually rode a bike to school, about one and a half miles, but if it was wet, he would drive his little Humber car. Mr Sinnott was a likeable man, tall and athletic with brown, closely cropped hair and soft brown eyes, that observed everything. Because this was a single classroom, it was amazing what we picked up from the other classes. I was in grade two in 1948, and there was only one other boy in the class with me. He was named Jacky and his brother Brian was the only other pupil in Graeme's class. We both sat beside these two brothers as class mates, right through till we went to our next school after our sixth year of primary. The desks were made to sit two pupils only.

Jacky and Brian were not the type of boys with whom we made good friends. Their family consisted of two older sisters at school and two younger ones not yet school age. Although ours and their families were the largest in the district, the Laity parents didn't join in any of the community activities like the school picnics, or the annual school concert. I only ever saw their parents once when I went with Brian to his house the day we ran away from school. The house was on the edge of the bush, with trees hiding it from public view, about half a mile from the main road and two and a half miles due south from where we lived. A large pile of beer bottles was stashed outside the back door. The bare wooden floors and unpainted walls, both indicated the family's poverty. Brian cut me a thick slice of stale bread which we spread with jam and washed down with a cold glass of water. His shy mother lingered in the background with two smaller girls. As soon as we finished our bread and water, I thanked Mrs Laity and Brian told her we would go back to school and collect our bikes. Brian was untying his dog when his father came around the house and asked Brian what we were doing. When he told him, we ran away from school instead of doing extra work, his father laughed and swore about Mr Sinnott. I was glad to get away from the unhappy scene. We went rabbiting and Brian's little dog chased and easily caught a rabbit. Seeing him run and catch up to the rabbit was the highlight of the day for me as I thought ahead of what would be awaiting me when I eventually arrived home, and at school the next day.

There was strict discipline at school. For serious stuff the boys would get the strap on the hands, and or lines of writing at lunch hour or for homework. Our teacher had accused us of not reading when we were, and after we had eaten our lunch we were meant to go back and do some work for punishment. We ate our lunch but jumped the fence and ran away.

When we were going back to school to get our bikes, we saw Mr

Sinnott riding his bike home. Brian yelled some abusive words at him which would only make matters worse for us. I rode home as quickly as I could, but it was getting late by this time and Father was coming down the sandy track in the Packard to find me. I got a thrashing in the laundry and some words of wisdom as soon as we were home. Next day at school both of us got six cuts, as we called them, across our hands with the strap, and we spent the next week of lunch times doing the original punishment. Bucking the establishment was always worth a try, but it never did seem to work for me. Just as well I suppose, as the punishment was probably the necessary incentive to keep me from more daring stuff.

Highlights for me at school were the annual Saturday school picnics when people came from all the surrounding districts. Money prizes were given for first, second and third in races and competitions. While I was no good at these, the lost money that could be found on the ground the following Monday at school was far more rewarding. At night, after the picnic, the locals organised a ball in the local hall which was on the corner over the road from the school. We didn't attend them.

Inside the school room was a foyer where the coats and school bags were hung. The classroom had windows only at the end opposite the entrance. All the desks faced a wall with two large blackboards. A chip heater stood in the centre between the blackboards. The heater was kept burning on cold days and was also used to heat milk on frosty mornings which enabled us to have a hot chocolate drink at ten o'clock. It was good also for warming frozen hands on the hot mugs when it was frosty.

On the back wall there was a photo of the Royal Family. At that time, it was King George VI, Queen Elizabeth and their two daughters. A map of Australia, another of Victoria and a world map filled the hanging space on the wall. The teacher sat at a table towards the back, and it shifted depending on how many children there were. The lower classes were at the end near the door. The alphabet was printed across the top of our blackboard, with the letters in capitals and small printing and coloured chalk pictures of the symbol they represented. I got to know my letters from this. Neatness of work and writing were a very important part of the learning process. Spelling and times tables were tested every morning. These were marked, and if we slacked with them, we would usually be kept in at lunch time to do extra work. These daily routines continued till form two of secondary school. Health check-ups each week were important to make sure our hands, fingernails, knees, boots, were clean and socks were pulled up. I scored well in the fingernails only because I used to bite them, and they were always too short for any dirt to be lurking there.

When Norm Sinnott went to another position, we got a teacher from England who had just emigrated. He was Mr Hopkins or 'Hoppy'. He tried to teach us Aussie kids all things English and we rather hated it. He could not maintain discipline. Father was the School committee secretary at the time. The last straw in Hoppy's short tenure was when he was making us learn to play rugby. In the process, he knocked me over, ran over me and I got quite severe concussion. He didn't try to contact our parents, but just let me wander. I tried to ride my bike home, but it was a bit of a disaster. There was what seemed then a steep hill about half way home. I got almost to the top but felt tired, so lay down in the gutter and went to sleep. I remember David riding past me on his bike, having been sent by the teacher to tell our parents. I must have slept for another twenty minutes at least because when Father came in the car, I was riding my bike just a little further on and waved to him as he went past. He stopped just past me.

By that evening I was in Sale hospital and was there for three days. I remember waking up early one morning to hear on the radio the sad news of King George VI's death. My head ached for a month after coming home, so Mother kept me from school during that time. The teacher also got the sack because the parents took their kids out of the school and told the education authorities that they would keep their children home till a new teacher was found. I think it took a week. The new teacher, named Mr Murray, was very good.

Getting to school on time was always a problem for Malcolm and me, especially in winter. We got up with the minimum time to get ready for school, wash, eat breakfast, get a sandwich for lunch, out the door, onto the bikes and away. It took about twenty minutes to ride to school on the gravel road, though we didn't have watches to time ourselves. Coming home was much more leisurely. Often, we dawdled home, especially Malcolm and me. We developed tracks off the side of the road up the banks and would mostly take these at various places along the route. We would almost always stop at the creek to look for fish or throw things into the water. There were birds' nests and an abundance of wild flowers in the bush in the spring. So much to do when we arrived home, chores, or maybe a game of cricket or footy in the paddock near the house. Sometimes, we would get on the wooden swing Father had built for us on a gum tree, about one hundred yards from the house. It was a long swing that could take one to four boys at any one time.

I remember Reverend Green coming to the school most weeks for religious instruction. He was a short stocky man, dressed in his dark suit with a white starched collar on backwards, which saved him wearing a tie. All ministers or priests wore their collars like this to distinguish them or their rank. Our church didn't have ministers because they consider all men equal and it was rather strange for me seeing Mr Green at first. However, I liked him with his notable wrinkled face and receding hair. He told us of some of his time as a chaplain in the war and of God's protection for him during that time. He used to hand out a small hymn book and after we had sung a couple of hymns, we would read prayers in unison from the back of the hymn book. One of his favourites hymns was, 'There is a green hill far away, without a city wall, where the dear Lord was crucified, who died to save us all.' It became one of my favourites too.

In my last year of primary school, I found it difficult to have a time alone with the Lord each day. At the Christian camps I was encouraged to do this with the aid of Scripture Union notes to help me understand the Bible. I gave up having my regular time with the Lord because I thought it didn't make any difference in my life. For six or seven weeks, I remember going my own way and feeling more and more miserable. By the end of that time, I confessed to God that I was weak and helpless without Him. 'Into my heart, into my heart, come into my heart Lord Jesus. Come in today, come in to stay, come into my heart Lord Jesus,' was the song that reminded of the time I gave my heart and life to Jesus. I was sure again that He never left me in those five years that had passed. My fellowship with Jesus was again restored.

There was another verse from the Bible that Mother often quoted. At first it didn't make an impression on me, but when I had said or done something wrong, her oft-quoted words started to sink in.

> *Fix your thoughts on what is true, and honourable, and right, and pure, and lovely, and admirable. Think about things that are excellent and worthy of praise.* (Philippians 4:8)

If only I could have always been more careful of my actions and speech.

I really enjoyed primary school in many ways and it was fun. I don't remember any of us boys getting any great scholastic achievements, just a small prize here or there. David won a couple of trophies for his athletic abilities, but I think that was the only silverware to grace our home. Us six boys were pretty average.

The farm at Willung was the perfect place for us six boys to spend our pre-teen and teen years. We had the privilege of literally being on the doorstep of a bush of thousands of acres which had abundant wildlife. Being able to roam freely in the bush while watching God's wonderful creation in all four seasons of the year. In the spring I watched a pair of blue wrens as they built a nest in tall bracken not far from our front door. The mother laid three tiny eggs. I saw the baby chicks in their nest before they had any feathers. Their three wide-open beaks were about all I could see as they were expecting another feed from mum or dad. Next time I saw them they had developed feathers and were squeezed into the small nest as though they were leaving very soon. Two day later when I looked, they were gone. In the garden as shrubs developed, there were nests with goldfinches and occasional blackbirds. Starlings and sparrows were problem nesters in the buildings, as were swallows. There was one pair of swallows who built their mud nest high in the rafters of the cow shed. The thump and vibration caused by the diesel engine at milking times loosened their nest. When eggs were laid, the nest fell to the floor and smashed. These birds were persistent because they built five nests in the same place with the same results. After their five attempts the parent swallows must have gathered on the wires with all the other swallows. A few days later they all flew away. The two swallows who built five nests didn't have any offspring to take with them. I was saddened by watching their futile experience.

Magpies and mud-larks nested in the branches of gums while kookaburras and parrots nested in the hollow branches of old trees. The loud laughter of kookaburras was something that we heard several times a day as they flew around their territory. At nesting time magpies were very protective of their nest, and they would swoop at anything that moved up to three hundred yards radius from their nest. They could be quite vicious.

Another scary bird at nesting time was the spur wing plover. When I first went near their nest, one of them would pretend he or she had a broken wing and they would limp away from the nest to try and get me to follow. But while they are nesting and raising their chicks, they swoop at anything or anyone that came near, either an animal or human. They caused a great fuss until we were a couple of hundred yards away. This bird nests on the ground and lays three or four off-white eggs with brown spots, about the size of a small hen's egg. We were instructed to keep out of their way, and we did.

Bigger birds, like the emu, lived in the bush and in the winter a pair of them came onto our farm looking for grass to eat. Father was not happy because he said they ate a lot of grass. However, I think he forgave them. One Sunday we came back from church they were on the flat part of our farm with ten cute brown and white striped chicks. Over a period, we watched the chicks grow. When they were half grown and developed their adult feathers, we didn't see them again. We never did find a nest of these flightless birds but we learnt how quickly they could run. Once, while driving the car, there was a pair running beside us along the roadside at forty miles per hour. We slowed down to know how fast they were going.

There were a pair of mountain ducks which fed in the swampy places on the flats. At nesting time, they found a place in a hollow tree, several feet off the ground where they hatched ten baby ducklings. Malcolm met a pair with several chicks on the bush side of the rabbit proof fence. The chicks couldn't fly and the adults were leading them to water but the fence was the barrier. Further along was a gate which Malcolm opened and then coaxed them through and they waddled off to the creek, a quarter of a mile away.

The wild animals were almost as varied as the birds. There were pests like rats, rabbits and mice. Once a plague of mice caused a lot of damage to the hay, wheat and food that was stored for the pigs. The cats mostly kept the mice from the house though they would sometimes get in cupboards where the cats couldn't go and we would have to trap the mice. There were several snake species like the deadly tiger, the black, and the brown snake. All had different skin colours, especially on their belly. The tiger had beautiful markings, stripes of gold, yellow and orange, which gave him or her the name. Some would grow up to six feet long.

David was the main snake killer in our family, but there was one occasion when he and Graeme saw a snake so big that even David was too afraid to attempt a kill. The report is that when they arrived home a few minutes later both David and Graeme were as white as ghosts, and they saw their biggest snake ever – half the main road width – about ten feet long. David told me this later in his life when I asked him about the story. The 'white as ghosts', was how Mother later described the two boys' faces when they came rushing into the kitchen a few minutes after seeing the snake. Would our Mother tell a tall one?

It was on this same day that these three brothers, David, Jim and Graeme, were coming along a grassy track near the farm where the Basset family went to live, and Graeme got a snake caught in the back wheel of his bike. He jumped off the bike and had quite a scare. David was able to kill the snake. In the summer months we were always careful where we walked, though actual sightings per summer would be ten-twelve. Probably no more than five or six were killed in a season.

At school in early spring, we were playing cricket and lost the ball in some long grass behind the boys' toilet. Three or four of us were stomping around in the grass to find the ball and I stood on what I thought was the missing object. My hand took hold of a snake just for a few brief seconds as I fled the scene with yells and shouts. The teacher was called and with the stick, he killed a four-foot-six black snake. Fortunately, the snake was still in a state of hibernation, because a bite without attention would have killed me in a few minutes. We were twenty-five miles from the nearest hospital. I am scared of snakes.

While checking the rabbit traps on our northern boundary fence, I found a small kangaroo hanging on the fence with his nose and short front legs just touching the ground. He had missed his jump over the four-foot-six high fence and his back-jumping legs went between the two top wires tipping him forward. He must have pulled up with a sudden jerk as his flight through the air was terminated. I expect the bigger roo's jumped first and he followed them, but even an inch too low would have caused this. His feet and legs were badly scraped on the barbed wire. We had no idea how long he was there, so Father put him out of his misery.

There were also a few wombats and wallabies in the bush. The wallaby is a smaller and black version of the kangaroo. Unlike the roo, they travel alone and not in groups. The wombat moves around on its own too, but it digs a burrow for a home. The hole opening for their burrow is two foot six in diameter and is quite distinctive from the smaller fox or rabbit holes. Wombats also dig holes under wire netting fences to get where they want to go. They are nocturnal animals and have strong claws both front and back. There were some wombats on the boundaries of the farm for a couple of years after we came, but someone must have hunted them because there were none around when we left. In those days there was a bounty on their scalps, as there was on fox scalps, because of the alleged damage they caused farmers.

Foxes were a pest where hens or newborn lambs were concerned.

Some of our neighbours who kept sheep lost numbers of lambs to foxes. Our hens were attacked and killed by foxes on some occasions. Once when I opened the nest-box on the hen house, a fox jumped out and took off into the bush. He had killed four hens and fed on two. He was curled asleep in the nest-box waiting for his big feed to wear off.

It was quite rare to see a koala bear in a gum tree near our place. This sleepy animal only eats gum leaves of certain trees and then they sleep between branches that hold them from falling, quite high up in the tree. Once when Father was in a paddock cutting ferns, he saw a koala up the gum he was under. Malcolm and I came home from school, so we rode our bikes to the tree where the bear was sitting quite comfortably about ten feet off the ground, asleep. He opened his eyes when he heard us talking but was quite content to go back to sleep again. I only saw one more in all the time we were at Willung.

There were also the harmless little creatures of the bush. The sugar glider is about the size of a small rat, but with skin between front and back legs which, when the need was there, can be used like a wing to glide from tree to tree. This along with its smaller cousin, the feather tailed glider, is a nocturnal animals. There were ring-tailed possums whose nests could be found in the bush and because they also were animals of the night, they were often at home in the daytime. Their tail could curl around a finger and they could hang from this.

Along with snakes were skink lizards by the dozen, blue-tongued lizards and the large goanna which could scale up a tree with ease. Their camouflage enabled them to hide as they were similar in colour to the tree bark. They loved eggs, and in the summer were occasionally found around the hen house. I wonder if God gave them the ability to know the cackle of the hen after she laid an egg? These large reptiles grew to six or seven feet and were expert tree climbers because they had very sharp claws.

The rabbit was a cuddly little animal and was a major pest to the farmer. They bred so quickly. As boys we were all taught how to use gin traps to catch them. These traps had two serrated steel jaws, which sprang shut when the bunny stepped on the open plate. The plate and the whole trap, was buried just under the ground in a place we knew the rabbit would come. The trap was attached to a chain and a steel peg which was hammered into the ground. All the ground around was made to look as if it hadn't been disturbed. When the rabbit got caught, he would twist and turn and at least have a very sore leg. Sometimes their leg would be broken off and just the stump would be left. At other times a fox would hear the rabbit squeal when he was caught and would come and have an easy-to-catch meal. However, mostly we came along morning and evening and found a rabbit squatting beside the trap. He would again try to escape, but there was a quick and efficient way to dispatch this little creature. We would put them in a bag and on our return home, would skin them. The skins were put on a U-shaped wire to dry and these we sold for a shilling or two each. The rabbit meat was either meat for us, or food for the dogs. Gin traps were a cruel method to catch rabbits. If rabbits were not so destructive to the whole land, we could easily feel sorry for them.

Another method of rabbit destruction was a fumigation bomb which when the fuse was alight, was placed as far down the rabbit hole as we could get this fizzing, smoking, little square box. Then, as quickly as we could we filled all the holes where the pungent smoke was coming out. The rabbits effectively dug their own grave. Father purchased a ferret once. We had several nets to put over the rabbit holes before the ferret was let down the burrow. He only ever got us three rabbits at any one day. Personally, I hated the sneaky, slimy, stinking animal, and was glad when he went to the animal hunting ground. He was more bother than his value.

I didn't like to see any animal suffer. An old cat lost hair off her back and her teeth were not in the best state. No one else in the family would put her down, so I took things into my own hands. I was the worst shot with any rifle in our family. I took her into the bush with Father's old rifle and put some food down for her. While she was eating, I aimed the rifle at her head, shut my eyes and pulled the trigger. When I opened my eyes, there was no cat in sight. Three days later she walked into the house. Cats are very forgiving.

The creek collected the runoff water for the land from Gormandale and the hills beyond. In the summer it was a small stream especially as more and more farmers started various irrigation projects up stream. However, the worst flood I saw had water about a three-feet deep, where it flowed over the banks of the creek and spread out at least four hundred and fifty yards wide. We watched from the hill at the back of our house as the flood waters spread to the neighbour's fences and the posts popped out one by one with the wire still attached to them. Fifteen minutes later, further down-stream on our side of the creek, the same thing happened with the boundary fence between us and the neighbour.

Three of us inquisitive boys jumped on our bikes and raced along the half mile of sandy track, turned left at the mail box, downhill towards the bridge and creek. It was an amazing sight. We were too stunned to say anything for a few moments as we watched the gurgling water in its rush to be first in line over the next obstacle. The roar of the creek was quite deafening as we were used to bird song as we normally travelled this way. The fast speed and the depth of water was quite a shock. I could hardly believe that the water was this high and flowing so fast. When we rode over the bridge three days ago, the water was fifteen feet below us. Now it was washing over the roadway on top of the bridge. The swollen creek washed away the rock filling from both ends of the bridge and even when the water receded, the road would be closed until it was made safe again. We wouldn't be able to get to school and the neighbours over the other side of the flooded bridge, were cut off from any access to shops and supplies.

But, the men of the district fixed up a flying fox over the worst of the flood waters to get supplies across the broken gap. This was used for two weeks until the road was opened again. Father spent a lot of time going to the shops, seven miles away in Rosedale to get supplies for the stranded neighbours. He would then tie them securely to the flying fox and send them across to those waiting on the other side. I went with him in the old Packard the first day after the flying fox was operational. The road was badly washed away in several places and Father got out to make sure the old bus could get through. We couldn't have turned around anyway, there was no room on the washed-out road. However, it was a tight squeeze through. There was no dust that day.

It was surprising how quickly things were back to normal again after the bridge was fixed. A month after the flood, the casual observer would not have noticed or been able to describe what I experienced in seeing the destruction and raw power of our quiet little creek. For a ten-year-old boy this was an unforgettable, awe-struck memory.

In the summer the creek was a place where we enjoyed fishing and swimming. For swimming we tried several holes along the creek but settled on one which had a log across at the downstream end. It was eight yards by two yards and deep enough to dive off the bank. We taught ourselves to swim at that place. One very hot day when our parents were away, Graeme and I spent several hours at the swimming hole in the middle of the day. We both got very badly sunburnt, a first and last time for me. It was several days before my back and shoulders were totally comfortable again.

One summer when our cousin Ted James was staying with us, Graeme caught a monster eel. Well, we thought he was a monster anyway. It took all three of us to haul him up the bank, and then cutting his head off to kill him was a major effort with only a pocket knife. Eventually, this was done. We took turns to carry this monster home in a sugar bag held over our shoulder. He was three feet long and weighed eleven and half pounds. When our story was related to others who lived on the creek, we could hardly believe the big eel stories that came to light. Everyone caught a far bigger eel than Graeme's. After this, swimming in the muddy creek water was a little less pleasant. What if one of these monsters fancied a boy's big toe for dinner?

I should tell my side of another yarn that my brothers to this day laugh at. I must admit that after seventy years I still get a chuckle when I think about it. It was in the winter, and David, Jim and Graeme were milking and feeding the pigs one evening when they hatched a plot to scare me. Mother and Father, Malcolm and Pete were not at home, and my job was to cook the evening meal and keep the house clean. It was dark outside and the meal was ready to be served. There was a knock on the front door, so I went and cautiously opened it enough to see three masked men standing there with a gun pointing in my direction. Hasty muffled words, 'Your money or your life,' reached my hot, scared ears. I slammed the door in their faces and fled out the back door and towards the cowshed yelling as I went. There was no sign of my brothers until above my shouts I heard them roaring with laughter behind me. In my youth, my scares were many, but this was the biggest so far. Well, I also put some of my acting skills together and that night they dished their own food, did the dishes, and clean up before they went to bed. I pretended to be so mad with them and was surprised that they fell for it. I am glad now we can all laugh about it. If I had been looking on, it would have been hilarious. By the way, the .22 rifle they pointed in my direction was not loaded.

It was always a good sign to see the yellow wattle tree flower in late winter. This told us that spring was almost ready to show forth its beauty of many colours, especially in the garden and the bush. The wattle was a favourite of mine with its masses of little yellow balls of fluff so close together, covering each tree. The trees in full bloom were a great sight of golden yellow flowers after a cold, grey winter. There were orchids that usually grew in a shady place. The one we called 'eggs and bacon' was the most colourful, in yellow and brown colours. Others were in green only and were shaped like a parrot's beak with a beard for a tongue. They would close like a trap when an insect landed there. We touched them too and they quickly snapped shut. Another one was a five-petal deep blue flower that smelt like chocolate and only grew to six or eight-inches tall. A rare round mauve flower with a two-inch circumference, had an exquisite fringe of short cotton-like threads which grew around the outer edge of the petals. However, these flowers were only out during spring and very early summer. They would soon die off when the hot dry weather came, or when a bush fire roared through and removed all trace of their short, beautiful life. One hot Sunday this is what happened to us.

Smoke was everywhere. Parents and older brothers were shouting orders and rushing around as though the world was on fire. Our world *was* on fire. My nine-year-old body was doubled over coughing and trying to breathe. Thick billowing smoke engulfed our weather-board house in a grey-white mass. It happened so quickly.

Yesterday was a hot normal summer's day, with a pleasant cool easterly breeze in the afternoon. Today was Sunday, and when we got up this morning, a dry northerly wind was stirring in the trees on the bush-clad hill in front of our isolated farm house. We left church as soon as it finished. There was bush fire smoke in the air and the smell brought anxiety to every farmer in the church. Father called us six boys to the car.

'Get in quick,' he said. 'Our house might be burnt down by the time we get home.'

The smoke haze was all around. We went around the corners on the gravel road faster than ever before over the nine miles to home. It was tense and exciting. Three miles from home we could see the billowing smoke on the other side of the wide valley. Our house was nestled against the bush fifty yards from where the fire would burn if it just kept to the bush.

Loud clear orders were given from the front seat as Father went even faster. Three weeks ago, we had laughed and joked through a fire drill on Saturday morning. Now it was real. We must get home.

'Will Ginger be dead?' I asked.

My brothers all laughed.

'Your cat can look after himself,' said Mother, with a forced chuckle.

Father glanced across at her. She brushed a tear away.

As we drove over the creek and up the hill where the bush started, we were all stunned by the destruction. No one spoke. We turned off the main road onto the narrow sandy track that led to our house, half-a-mile-away. Both sides of this track were blackened smouldering remains of where the fire had recently passed. Everywhere, and everything was black and bare. Was our house like this?

This morning, as we travelled the other way, the ferns scratched against the car on both sides. A rabbit ran across the road in front of us, and just as we turned onto the main road, a black snake slithered across the gravel into the bracken. No sign of any animals or birds now. Logs were burning brightly. The bark on the gums was still glowing and smoking. It was a black stark scene. Dark grey ash littered the sandy track from burnt leaves.

Silence. No one could speak.

I thought of all the animals in the bush, the kangaroos, birds, rabbits, possums, koalas and even the lizards and snakes. Some I saw recently. A few weeks ago, I watched three baby blue wrens as they flew from their tiny nest in the bracken ferns near the house. I wondered where they would be now. They would have no home tonight. We may not have a home either.

This morning Mother asked me to help set the dining table in the lounge for the special tea we enjoyed on Sunday nights. The Royal Doulton dinner set was used on a clean starched table cloth, with eight small plates and special silverware to go with them. Mother picked three red rose buds to go in a small glass vase in the table centre. Her beloved pedal organ was on the far side of the lounge, beside a small writing desk which kept her poetry and letter writing things and a tin of ancient and new family photos. We loved searching through them, especially our own baby photos.

In the bottom three drawers of the desk Father had all his tax papers, insurance records, and the farm books which told him how profitable the farm was. He often talked about wishing he could afford more insurance. I wondered if he was thinking that now. Mother stared straight ahead.

Father broke the silence. 'We may not be able to get home'. He choked on his words just for a moment. 'We may need to leave the car before we get to the fire face, and hurry home from there across the paddock.' All eyes peered forward as we came over the second last low hill. At the bottom the fire front was raging. Flames were shooting high in the air. They would burst up and then die down. There was a regular low flame about three feet high that snaked its way up and over the high hill on the left. We were travelling at ninety degrees to this wall of flame. Smoke billowed around and the fire smell penetrated the car and our Sunday best clothes.

'Thank goodness, it has not reached the house yet,' said Mother. 'We may be able to save some things.'

'No time for that,' said Father. His voice was sharp. 'All of us must work outside to save the house.'

More silence, except for the dull noise of the purring Packard engine.

'Wind all the windows up now. Sparks might blow in,' Father said. His voice loud and urgent.

The smoke filled all the view of the track ahead as we came closer to the fire. The old car slowed. It was hot and stuffy inside now. We inched forward. As we neared the flames Father saw that we could just sneak past, as the flames on the right were about twenty feet ahead of those on the left. It was very hot.

'Hold tight,' he said, as the old car swerved one side and then the other, spurting past the flames and through a thick wall of smoke.

'Phew,' Father said. 'That was close.' The tension eased just a little.

Up the hill I watched as large gum bust into a huge fireball that shot flames fifteen feet into the air. Trees would suddenly burst into high flaming torches as the heat and flames caught the volatile eucalyptus leaves. Sparks showered off them as the hot wind swirled around.

Now we were ahead of the fire wall, but the smoke was much thicker. It was everywhere.

'The house is still there,' said Mother as we crested the last rise in the track. 'Thank You Lord,' she added, her voice almost a whisper.

'We may just be able to save it,' Father said as we drove past the blackwood tree near the start of the bush track, a right-hand turn through the gate and out into a clear paddock away from the fire and house.

'All out. Be quick,' he yelled as he braked the car to a sudden stop.

We all tumbled out and ran to the house. The fire was coming quickly now. We raced around to get sorted for the onslaught and heat. The dense smoke swirled around.

'Get rags and tie them over your nose and mouth,' Mother yelled as we rushed to our duties.

'Quick, help me with this hose. Hurry up.' Her voice was desperate.

Water buckets were moved and empties put under the tap in their place. The grey-blue smoke carried burnt leaves swirling around and landing anywhere. Dark masked figures would emerge like black ghosts in a fog collecting water or going to another spot. Everyone was rushing around. As the wind shifted the smoke momentarily, I could see the flames getting closer to the house. Mother kept the hose spraying the walls that with the heat and wind would soon dry again.

Father rushed to start fires along the bush perimeter nearest the house. This was to burn back to the main fire wall. David and Pete were helping him. The wind and fire noise made it hard to hear. The smoke kept coming and blocked clear views of everything.

Mother yelled, 'I think the old blackwood is about to go.'

This tree was on the edge of the bush. Flames licked its trunk and then up into the dense leaves. It fired with a loud bang. A huge wall of thick smoke came billowing across the seventy-yards between it and the house. The whole house was engulfed in thick grey-white choking smoke. I doubled over trying to grasp air. I was coughing, crying and choking for air as I staggered around. My eyes were stinging from the smoke. Mother was troubled too. She had dropped the hose to clear her eyes. Then the smoke cleared and we could breathe easier. The work was hot and exhausting. Slowly the thick smoke drifted away, though the battle was not over yet. Pete and David were using old wet sacks on a handle to beat out hot spots of fire. Graeme and Jim still ferried water in buckets for the others across no-man's-land towards the fire. After several minutes the fire moved on from the blackwood to leave it a black shell of branches and the trunk still burning.

'Hurray! It's gone,' shouted Mother as she slumped exhausted on the front step.

The fire was still close, but it passed the house and was racing forward gobbling up all in its path.

'Phew, said Father as he took off his hot sweaty cap and sat beside Mother. 'The house is saved and we're all safe. Are you okay?'

The other exhausted blackened family members appeared one by one on the veranda for a drink and to catch their breath.

'Boy! That was lucky,' said Malcolm.

'Did you see how high the flames were? It was so hot and scary,' said Graeme.

'The smoke and flames were unbelievable especially from the blackwood tree,' said Father. 'That'll be the end of her.'

Mother, her eyes filled with tears, quietly turned away and went inside. The blackwood was her favourite tree.

The fire raged through the bush for two more days and nights before we had rain. Our lovely bush was all blackened and bare, with only the tall trees having any leaves left. Little spots here and there missed being burnt but the birds and animals were all gone. For a couple of years after that we always got blackened when we got firewood from the bush, but the first good rain started the re-growth. The gums recovered remarkably with new fresh leaves growing up their trunks and on their branches. As the growth returned so did the animals and birds. The next spring there were an amazing array of orchids that came to flower among the new bracken that was growing again from its hairy underground roots.

We didn't have a big noisy party or a celebration that Sunday night of the big smoke, but we did have the meal Mother had pre-pared, eaten using her best sets of crockery and cutlery. Afterwards, Father gathered us together in the lounge and read a few chosen verses from his Bible from the thirteenth chapter of Hebrews 5 and 6,

Don't love money; be satisfied with what you have. For God has

*said, 'I will never fail you. I will never abandon you.' The Lord is
my helper, so I will have no fear. What can mere people do to me?*

And verse 14:

*For this world is not our permanent home; we are looking forward
to a home yet to come.*

We all knelt beside our chairs while Father thanked God for caring
and protecting us and our home. Before I went to sleep that night,
I had the assurance that God always cares for me and I tried to
imagine what kind of home I had to look forward to.

Graeme and I went to the Technical School in Sale. Graeme was
there a year before I went. We boarded in Sale with the Thompsons,
friends of our parents. On Friday nights we would catch the school
bus to Rosedale and Father would meet us there. We arrived home
at about 6pm. Monday mornings at 8am we would catch the bus
to go back to school.

City life was hard to take. Everything was so different. Each
night, fresh bread and milk were delivered by horse and cart. The
milk was ladled out of cans, as each household took out a container
to put it in. There was no sewage system in Sale then and very early
in the morning a man would thunder down the road in an old
truck and carry an empty bucket to each toilet and collect the full
one he had left there a week or so before. Polite people called him
the night watchman. This space doesn't permit all the other names
boys called him. It was considered one of the lowest jobs around.

Anyway, secondary school was a challenge for me. After being
used to one teacher, here we saw different teachers for each subject.
We had metal lockers to keep our books and gear in and carried a
key and made sure we locked the metal box or we would have stuff

stolen. That was new for me as was wearing a school uniform which we soon got used to, but after four years we were glad for a change.

I enjoyed those school years. There were practical subjects like wood work, metal work, engineering, pottery and art. In the academic subjects, I did maths, English, science, tech drawing and social studies which was supposed to be geography and history, but we didn't get the latter. After the second year we were able to select practical subjects, and I selected the carpentry side of things which included tech drawing. I loved wood and learnt how to use the tools properly, skills which I have continued learning. As part of English both Graeme and I were encouraged to take up debating. We both led debating teams in the school competitions. It was quite boring really, but I suppose we started to learn something about public speaking. Friday afternoon was our sports day each week. The choices were tennis, cricket, Aussie rules football and softball, which I selected. Graeme took cricket.

Graeme made a friend in his first year, and his brother became my friend in my first year. However, after my second year the brother's parents moved to Melbourne for the boy's education, and we missed them. We enjoyed weekends at each other's farms. Geoff and Robin's parents lived as far east from Sale as we lived west. Theirs was a sheep farm as opposed to our dairy farm. They had a bottomless waterhole which they swam in. Although I was thirteen years old, I was scared stiff at the thought of swimming in water where I couldn't see or stand on the bottom. Geoff, Robin and Graeme were quite happy to swim the forty yards across the pond and back again. If they could do it so could I! Halfway across, I thought of the water being bottomless and I was terrified. The side where my feet could touch the bottom was a welcome relief, but I knew I was to do the longest, short swim of my life all over again. It was a long way to a bridge, so I eventually took the plunge and swam my way back. For the next few years, whenever I suffered a bad dream it would be about sinking into a bottomless hole. Fortunately, I always woke up before I set my feet on solid ground, if there was such a thing in dreams. Oh well, I had something that always reminded me of our otherwise happy visit to the Hill's farm.

Some of our teachers were unforgettable. Mr Forrester, who was nicknamed 'Chop-chop', taught science. Our social studies and English teacher kept his strap in his hip pocket, but soaked it in vinegar or alcohol to make it harder. He used it on me a couple of times, once for just turning around. It was hands open, one on top of the other held together in front. He held the wrist with his left hand and delivered the strap with his right. Our hands were changed over after each stroke, and six was the maximum delivered at any one time. He was the only person to discipline me in that way in my four years at Tech and each time there were only two strokes.

When I was fifteen, I started to consider my spiritual life quite seriously. I knew that if I was to progress in my Christian life it was no use sitting back and just drifting along. People needed to see Jesus living in my life. I wrote away for a Bible correspondence course, which when completed, gave me a greater basic understanding of God's holiness, the work of Jesus and the person of the Holy Spirit, sin and its consequences, heaven and hope we have in the return of Jesus taking us to be forever in our heavenly home. While I learnt about all these things at Sunday School and church, they became much more real to me by having them reinforced and letting the Lord speak to me through the Scriptures. It was about this time I asked one of the elders at church if I could be baptised. The day of the baptism was remembered for two main reasons: it was a freezing cold winter's day at the creek where I was baptised, and the verse was given to me,

Trust in the Lord with all your heart; do not depend on your own understanding. Seek His will in all you do, and He will show you which path to take. (Proverbs 3:5-6)

One hundred and ten years before our old black Packard rattled along the sandy drive to the Willung farm, our ancestor made a much more difficult journey. James Knowles was eighteen years old when he was sentenced in England as a convict Number 680, to transportation on the sailing ship *Layton* to Hobart, Tasmania in 1838. While working as a ploughman in Lancaster, England, he stole a heifer, possibly for something to eat. He was tried on the 22nd of October 1838 and was given a sentence of ten years. James was imprisoned until the ship left England in May 1839, arriving in Hobart on the 8th of December the same year. Records taken from documents we have, show James committed his crime in 1837 and it was two years later before he arrived at Hobart. He was described as a twenty-year-old, five-feet-ten-inches tall, with light brown hair. He had a round face with blue eyes and sallow complexion. The *Layton* took about six months to make the journey halfway around the world. This man was to become our great-great-grandfather, and one of the early settlers in Tasmania.

We cannot uncover details about where he was held or much else, but documentation tells he was convicted of being drunk on the fifth of October 1846 and fined five shillings, and his release from the original sentence was the fourth of July 1847. We have no record of ten years after his release. The marriage register does describe James as being a widower. Was he married during those ten years and his wife died, or was he married before he left England? Tasmania had no law for registration of births or marriages at that time.

Helen Muir comes on the scene ten years after his release. She was a twenty-one-year-old illiterate immigrant from Scotland. Her assisted passage aboard the *Forrest Monarch* in 1857 cost her sixteen pounds. I assume James and Helen worked on the same farm because John, their firstborn son, arrived in 1859. Their other children to follow were Henry, George, Frank, William, James, Septimus, Duncan and Agnes, in that order. We don't know the date they moved to the Sheffield district. We know however, that the move was at least five years before Agnes was born.

There was no mechanisation or paved roads. Horses and bullock teams were the means of clearing the dense bush. Single furrow ploughs were pulled by one or two horses in harness. One of the older boys drove the horses and worked the plough. The lead horse would walk in the furrow caused by the plough the last time round. Personal transport was by horse and one's own legs until formed roads made horse and buggy possible. People would ride or walk for miles to go to church, to town or to visit someone.

In 1874 James Knowles started a new chapter in his life. Two evangelists came from England named Brown and Moyse. They held Bible teaching meetings in the district. It was at one of these meetings that James came to faith. He was fifty-four years old. Some of his family came to know the Lord also. These details are in the book by Alan Dyer, *God Was Their Rock,* written about people in the area.

John was fifteen when he became a follower of Jesus. Like his father his life was changed forever. John was to become my great-grandfather. One of his dramatic experiences is told in *God Was Their Rock*. John was on his horse crossing the flooded Dasher river. The surging waters swept him off the horse. He managed to grab hold of the horse's tail and it swam to the riverbank pulling an exhausted, waterlogged owner with it. Lucky John.

When he was twenty-two years old, he married Mary Bryon and registered his marriage in June 1881 in Launceston. John's marriage was recorded before his parents registered their marriage. James and Helen officially married in Launceston at the Baptist minister's house in October 1881 where James is recorded as being sixty-one years old and Helen forty-three. They had all nine children by this time.

John and Mary inherited the family farm, lived there while over the next several years they raised five of their own children. They were Ada Maude, Caroline Mary, Grace, James Henry and John William. John and Mary worked the family farm in Beulah and they were still there in 1902. Later they moved to Spreydon. John died there in 1927.

James Henry, also known as Jim, was the fourth child in the family. My grandad was born on the 13th of September 1887. Grandad was brought up in a Christian home and he went to church and Sunday School as well as having his basic primary education.

Grandad, James Henry, married Grandma, Ethel Priscilla Holloway in 1909. The Holloways were not a local family but had emigrated from England and settled on the east coast of Tasmania at St Helens. Ethel was the third of twelve children and her mother's maiden name was Louisa Annie Diprose. The record of her descendants can be found on pages 173 to 205 of *Go Be Fruitful and Multiply*.

Percy James, their first child, was born on the 7th of January 1910. After him came Florence, and then Minnie. By the time Minnie was born, the First World War was two years in progress and Grandad had volunteered for service in the army. He signed up in August 1916 and went to Hobart for initial training before being shipped to England in October 1916. He experienced fighting in the trenches in Belgium and France and if he hadn't been wearing his steel helmet, he wouldn't have returned home alive. He got the mumps and measles while away and was on the front line when mustard gas was used. A shell exploded quite close to him. A piece of shrapnel went through both his cheeks smashing his new set of dentures, but leaving both his cheek bones intact. Later a steel helmet saved his life when it was knocked off his head but seconds later, another bullet gashed his upper left arm. He wrote before going into the trenches in one of his preserved letters to Ethel, 'No matter what happens to me I am in the safest keeping possible because God watches over me.'

After his discharge from hospital, he was sent back to his main job of boot repairing. Grandad was a cobbler by trade. He was away from his family for three years while he and many other troops waited for a ship to take them home. Their ship eventually arrived in Melbourne about the middle of October, 1919. He told us little of his terrible experience. Wilbur, their youngest, was born in 1922.

Grandad left a small country store in Kimberley to go to war and on his return, continued with this business. It didn't seem to be very profitable owing to the size of the surrounding community and the poor state of the economy of the country at that time. He was a battler and could turn his hand to most things. In 1939, before World War II, Grandad and Grandma moved to Victoria and settled on a small holding they purchased about three miles south of Neerim South. In 1944, our parents moved to Victoria and rented a house which Aunty Flo and Uncle Col eventually bought. The house, on one-hundred-and-sixty acres of land, was about half a mile from any neighbours and a mile from where Grandad lived.

In later times, Grandad and Grandma built themselves a small cottage in the valley beside their daughter Flo and her family. They lived there till their deaths, and it seemed to me that they had money for little except for the basics. When they built the house, it was in the middle of the bush and a lot of logging trucks passed by on the gravel road. Later, the property was cleared for farming. All around, the tall gums on the hills have gone and cattle graze where trees used to flourish.

I remember slipping and sliding on the dirt track to their place on the wet occasions when we visited them. I was never close to Grandad, but he was always pleasant, and it was always good to see how he had a knack of fixing or making things with his hands.

Our father, Percival James Knowles, was named after his maternal grandfather. Most of his early life was spent in Kimberley where his parents owned a family store until they moved to Spreydon, about four miles from Devonport. Percy was a businessman at heart but had no formal training or education. He married Mother on Christmas day 1934 when he was almost twenty-four. They had a five-year engagement because of the Great Depression years, which left many people around the world without work or income. Five pounds was all our parents had left in the bank after their marriage. They went to St Helens on the east coast of Tasmania to be near his parents, who moved there some time before. Father took a job as a Rawleigh salesman after his marriage. He remained in this job for six years. His territory stretched all around the east coast, from Hobart to Launceston in the west, to Scottsdale in the north. It seems he was often a couple of weeks away from home at a time. His car was a 1928 Chrysler. He later talked with a lot of affection for that car and the numerous bogs and hard places he went. He was a careful driver all the time I knew him, and I expect all his life. At some stage they moved to Paratta near the centre of Tasmania. Jim and Graeme were born while they lived there. They had moved to Bagdad before I was born in 1941. Malcolm was also born while we lived there.

On the 10th of February 1941, Father signed up as a volunteer for the army. That was the same day of Graeme's first birthday. I am not sure of the significance of that date, although there was a lot of pressure from the government to get more men for the army. Father was not sent overseas, but was kept in a clerical position in the army headquarters which was in Brighton. To be closer to where he was based, the family moved to Bagdad which today is about an hour's drive from Hobart on the main road north.

Our maternal grandparents met while working on a farm near

Timaru in New Zealand. Our Grandpa was born in Christchurch in 1877 and given the name John James Whitley. The earliest record I have is their marriage register which is dated the 26th of December 1905 when he married Clare Elliott. It is recorded that Grandpa was a mechanic by trade and was married when he was twenty-eight. His parents lived in Dunedin. My great-grandpa was named James Whitley married to Margaret, nee McBride. They had two boys in the family. Our Grandpa John – Pa Whit as we called him – had another brother called Henry, but I have no record of him. Their father remarried when their mother died when John and Henry were relatively young. Their new step-mother gave John and Henry a hard time according to what John told his own son Geoff. Uncle Geoff wrote an undated letter and gave me this piece of information about his father's early childhood. Parents in those days were reluctant to give too much information, so that's all I have gleaned.

Our maternal Grandma, Clara Ethel Elliott was born in the Huon Valley south of Hobart in December 1879. Her father was one of eleven children of John Elliott who, with his wife, emigrated to Tasmania in 1837 on the *William Metcalfe*. Clara's father was born in 1844 and died in 1884 when Clara was five years old. He left a young family of five living children. Two other children were born in the family, but they died soon after their births.

Clara was single when she moved with her married sister to New Zealand to be a nanny for her sister's young children. Later Clara worked on a large farm near Timaru as a nanny to three children. While there she met her future husband, who was the chauffeur and mechanic on the same farm. The records show that John Whitley and Clara Elliott were engaged for two months and then married. Their wedding took place in Clara's sister home in Timaru. Soon after their marriage, they moved to Devonport, Tasmania and so did her sister and brother-in-law. It seems that things didn't work out well for them in Timaru.

Our mother, Ella Faith Whitley was born on the 16th of November 1906 in Devonport, Tasmania. Ella was quite small when the family moved to Camperdown in Victoria where they stayed for four years before moving back to Devonport. They bought a property with a house and enough room for Pa Whit's large workshop at 32 Turton Street, Devonport. The property backed on to Smith Street, which ran parallel to Turton Street. There were six children in the family: Ella, Harry, Marion, Clare, Geoff and Charles (who died as a baby).

Mother had a primary education and wanted to go to secondary school, but finance in the family didn't allow for that. In those days the basics were strongly taught in school and Mother learnt them well. She learnt to play the organ and along with that came singing. Their parents took the children to church and Sunday School, where Mother taught a class when she was old enough. They used to walk everywhere they went, that included church and Sunday school, the beaches and the shops. Devonport was a good town to grow up in. Mother found work in a shoe shop when she left school and she was in this kind of occupation until her marriage.

Mother went from a prosperous town, Devonport, to a small out of the way town on the east coast – St Helens. She had grown up in Devonport where all her own family and support network was there. She also went to be near her in-laws. There was no electric power where they lived, and no hot running water. Toilets were outside. Fires were all wood-burning both for heating and cooking. Mother got help to do some of the housework when the family increased.

It was from this pioneering spirit that us six boys were descended, and this may have given us the ability to enter the early years of our lives with a great sense of adventure. We knew very little of our relatives' history at that time. The reason for our enjoyment of the Willung farm, was probably because we enjoyed all the things in

God's creation, and the adventurous spirit of past generations was always something to be admired.

I appreciate knowing that I am a small part of the fifth generation of these families, and all my grandparents back to James and Helen were followers of Christ or Christians. James Knowles started his journey of faith when he was fifty-four years old. While the men in this family were Christians, their wives also made their own individual and personal commitment to Jesus as the Son of God. These women from other than the Knowles family, made a tremendous contribution to the wisdom and knowledge their families gained from having Christian parents. Our own mother and her mother also, held their families together at certain times in their lives. I know our Grandma Knowles did too, especially during the war years and just after. It is a great privilege to be brought up in a home where God has first place, and the stories and teachings of the Bible are taught and encouraged. The Christian influence in our family has kept us relatively free from many of the influences that cause much sorrow in the community at large.

Who would have thought that a convict, born in England in 1820 and transported to serve his time in Tasmania, would meet an illiterate emigrant girl from Scotland, who arrived twenty years after him (Helen was eighteen years younger than James), and that I would be linked to this man and woman? Or who could think of such a plan that I would be related to John Elliott, who came with his wife as emigrants from England to Tasmania in 1837. They had eleven children, one of them born in 1844 became the father of my maternal grandmother, Clara Elliott, who was only five when her father died. Or, who could think of a plan for Clara Elliott to meet John Whitley in Timaru, New Zealand and Clara, returning to Tasmania with her newlywed husband, would have a firstborn daughter called Ella Faith Whitley who would later marry Percy Knowles. I became their fifth born son. No one but God, could plan something like this, to get all the timing and other minute details right for those hundred and fifty years, so that my birth date was just as God planned. I was right where He wanted me and in the family of God's choice for my development. God was loving me so much that He thought of me before He made the world.

Ephesians 1:4-5 says,

Even before He made the world, God loved us and chose us in Christ to be holy and without fault in His eyes. God decided in advance to adopt us into His own family by bringing us to Himself through Jesus Christ. (NLT)

The Bible has become my guide as I have journeyed through life. In Psalm 32:8 the Lord says,

I will guide you along the best pathway for your life. I will advise you and watch over you. (NLT)

Could I want for anyone better than the Almighty God who every moment guides me, advises me and watches over me?

CHAPTER 4

We spent six happy years at Willung and they seemed to have passed by so quickly without us even taking note that six years were added to our lives. Pete was a young man almost out of his teen years with his driving licence and car of his own. While our parents were wondering what they should do with their growing boys, Father received an unexpected letter from the Soldier Settlement Commission asking him why he hadn't been applying for the farms that were advertised for resettlement. They asked our parents to go for an interview in Melbourne to answer any questions they may have and to clarify the situation for them. Father told them that because he hadn't gone overseas on active duty, he thought he wasn't eligible to apply for a farm. Father and Mother came away with the good news that they were indeed eligible to apply for advertised farms. The government was making these available on long term loans at a very low interest rate. A new house would be built, new sheds and all the material for fences and a milking plant would be provided. Money was also available for purchasing a herd of cows. With this information my parents were clearly seeking God's will in the matter. They thanked Him and continued to pray.

Our parents first arranged a meeting with Alex Ronalds, and while he was very sorry to see us go, he knew that this move would be the best for our family. He asked Father if he could recommend someone for the job, and told him to raise some extra calves so we could take these with us when we moved. The daily newspaper and the *Weekly Times* were diligently searched by Father and Mother for Soldier Settlement farm ads. The first one that came up was near Casterton, about three-hundred-and-forty miles west of Willung. Should they move that far away to somewhere we were completely unfamiliar with? Would it have good schools and churches? Would they have peace about it? They decided they should go and see what was on offer, taking Malcolm and me with them.

We drove all the way to Casterton but it was not the sort of country we thought suitable for dairy farming. None of us fell in love with the farms. It was late in the afternoon so we looked for a place to camp overnight. The next day we travelled back to Willung.

About a month later, we were on our way to Mirboo North to see some more farms that came up for ballot. Mirboo North was two hours away from Willung and what we saw, we liked. Father sent off the papers applying for the five farms we liked best. The township was a small, clean and well-kept in an undulating setting of green pasture. The farms had some trees on them and were not so blank and stark as the ones we saw near Casterton. We waited expectantly for a reply, but our application was declined.

At Nambrok – half an hour's drive from home – some farms were being developed on land previously used for sheep and beef cattle. The district measured an average rainfall of twenty-two inches a year, which was not enough rain for dairy farming. The government built a dam about twenty miles away. It captured a lot of runoff water from the distant mountains. Miles of channels were needed to run the water from the dam to the prepared farms for flood irrigation. Up to ten farms were put up for ballot at a time and Father applied again but was unsuccessful. A second letter came from the Soldier Settlement Commission asking Father for another interview. After that interview Mother and Father seemed much more relaxed about getting a farm. Some more were advertised at Nambrok and when they put in their application, they were allocated the first choice of what was on offer. Later, they were told that it was one of the best farms out of over more than a hundred in the area.

It could not have been better for us as a family. The future for our parents looked secure as they gave thanks to the Lord for His provision. We didn't need to change shops, or banks, schools, churches, or other places where we were known. There was about three months before we needed to move to our new situation. I thought of the journey the Lord directed us on through this period. Even in the ups and downs of wondering if we would get this farm or that, God selected just the right one for us. This helped me to know that genuine, trusting in the Lord with all my heart, was the right path for my future.

We moved to Nambrok in July 1956. I recently turned fifteen and was half way through my third year at Sale Technical College. I have no recollection of the move except we moved into an old house on our new farm surrounded by cypress trees, with a barn-like shed at the back and an orchard on the south side. The house was unoccupied for about two years and that musty smell of dampness of neglected houses was evident. It became our home for almost a year, as the new house was not yet built. The land was still being prepared for sowing the grass seed. This large solid old homestead was situated in about the middle of the property. Five of us boys were still at home, Pete was away at least three weeks of the month with a herd testing job, but there was always a bed for him on his days off. This new farm was situated about fifteen miles from the Willung farm and became a major turnaround for our parent's financial security.

There were aspects of the previous farm we missed, especially the bush and the sense of freedom we enjoyed there. Here, if shooting was done it was usually to get a rabbit or hare or stray wild cat. At Willung we could shoot in the bush with freedom or cut wood to burn on the fire or for fence posts if needed. We could swim in the creek or go spot lighting for rabbits. We still did the latter, but it was different.

When we moved in, there were tractors working on our farm to get it ready for sowing grass seed before the summer came when it would need to be irrigated. Drains and watercourses for the irrigation were put in with bulldozers and tractors levelling and grading the paddocks. New fencing was erected after the grass seed was sown and before the cattle could be purchased. A new cowshed was being built near the road, the new house site was marked out and an implement-shed and a garage were built. A new windmill was assembled by a well near the old homestead together with a tank on a stand which gravity fed cattle troughs for each paddock. At first only sixty acres was ploughed and levelled for irrigation. The new cows were purchased and added to several that we pre-reared at Willung. We didn't have any pigs at Nambrok and sold whole milk when the milking started. The milk was put in stainless steel drums and taken out to a stand at the road each morning for collection. Later, a large vat was purchased to hold the milk and a tanker drove in near the cowshed and pumped the milk into the truck. This method was much more efficient.

In my third year at Tech – 1956 – Graeme and I were able to go to the Melbourne Olympic Games. It was an organised school trip by train for two hundred students plus several teachers. Graeme and I stayed with friends in Cheltenham and caught the suburban train into the cricket ground for two mornings. We enjoyed two full days at the games, an experience I will never forget. There were crowds of people jostling to get off the trains and into the stadium at the Melbourne cricket ground. We were two school boys among one hundred thousand other people who packed the place out by mid-morning. It was a spectacular sight.

We saw many of the different types of athletics, John Landy in the mile race, Betty Cuthbert with a world record in a woman's event and Shirley Strickland in the hurdles. We watched high jumping, pole vaulting, long-distance running events and the finish of the walking and marathon races. Our seats were in front of the start of the sprint races. We saw as one runner in the marathon come into the stadium ahead of all the rest but because of heat exhaustion he fell, got to his feet again and wobbled and fell again. After the third fall he was carried away and unable to complete the race. The crowd was stunned to silence. Two other athletes passed him while he lay on the track.

It was hard for me to properly settle at school in my fourth year of Tech even though we were much closer now as the bus ride was only about half an hour each way instead of the hour and a half to Willung. I loved all that was happening on the farm and it was slowly coming into shape. There was always lots of work to do. Even after school we generally were called on for milking, especially the year I started fourth form as the bus came right past our house. Graeme had left school by now and Malcolm was in his third year at Tech.

I watched with avid interest as our new home was being built. Mother was delighted with the finished product. There was a sleep-out at the old house which Father bought from the house removers. The sleep-out was put on skids and towed with the tractor to a close position beside the new house. It was of solid construction and was used by up to three of us boys as our room at various stages. It was my patch when I worked on the farm and my space too when I was at home before going to Hong Kong.

In the fourth form I took subjects that would lead me into the building or carpentry trade. I loved working with wood. However, as the year progressed it became apparent that I was going to be working on the farm as all the older brothers left for other fields of endeavour. Pete and Jim were herd testing, David got married and rented his own home, Graeme worked for the neighbour but then went to Melbourne to work in a bank. At the end of his third year at Tech, Malcolm left home for the big city too. He took an office job with a shipping/transport company. I slotted into farm life pretty well and enjoyed the challenges. It was a laid back lifestyle with the busy times in spring and summer with cows calving at the end of winter and harvesting of hay and irrigation to be kept up in summer. There was still fencing to be done, and trees to be planted for shelter belts along the boundary fences.

I gave up my hope of a carpentry/building job and took up farming. This became my work for the next three and a half years. I started at five pounds a week including board, but this was doubled by the time I left. The farm gave me a wide experience, building yards, gates and a hen house. There were fences to erect, concreting, paths to lay, harvesting hay with tractors, and the daily stuff of milking cows, feeding them hay in the winter, and flood irrigating the paddocks in the summer. There were weeds like thistles to eradicate, gardens and lawns to attend to around the house and a tree-planting programme for shelter belts for the cattle.

My holidays were mostly at Christian camps. In the summer it was Mornington, and three of us organised a local boys' camp under canvas at Wilsons Promontory, where we took twenty-five to thirty boys. They were memorable times for all of us. The last of these I attended was not long before I went to Hong Kong. We walked the ten miles to Wilsons Promontory lighthouse and back again. Twenty miles for a day. We were all very tired by the time we collapsed back into camp late that afternoon. What joy there was in camp that we made it there and back safely. I usually enjoyed the cooking at these camps. One year I had miscalculated the menu. For the last morning we were supposed to have eggs on toast after our porridge, but I used up all the eggs we needed. There were a few jars of stewed apple left over. So, with curry powder to give it a different flavour, I served curried apples on toast and I have never lived it down. The lads who were there, now all grown men, remind me of that breakfast if ever I meet any of them. Ah well! What would you have done?

The summer camps at Mornington, which I attended for a few years were mixed, with up to over a hundred young people in each. At first, they were in tents and marquees, but then a hall and dormitories and proper toilets were erected. In the beginning it was quite primitive, but people from all over Victoria attended and many of them became Christians. Some from isolated areas, grew in their faith and went into full time ministry either locally and overseas. The camps usually lasted a week. One year I took in three, one after another, but it took a while to catch up on myself after that. It was full-on work from early morning to late evening. At one camp I was asked to mentor a twelve-year-old from a broken home where his drunken father beat him. He was quite morose at first but slowly became more animated as the camp went on, and he made a couple of other friends with other boys too. I felt so inadequate for this task and I only hope that something we shared together in our conversations was a help to him. We made some interesting friends at the camp and some were invited to our farm for short stays, and in turn we visited them in their city situations. We learnt a little of city life and most of them enjoyed the freedom and quietness of our country living.

Among the families we met at the Mornington were the Thorsens.

They were a family of four with a girl, Eleanor, about my age and a boy named Bruce who was about two years younger than me. We often stayed with each other in the intervening years. At the camps their parents were known as Uncle Vic and Aunty Jean. Uncle Vic worked at International Harvester in Dandenong. They lived in Edith Vale, a suburb of Melbourne on the Mornington Peninsula, near their church at Bon Beach. Uncle Vic was a real encouragement to me. He was very active in his local church and he arranged for me to go with him one Sunday afternoon to a ministry called 'bus work'. This was what several Brethren churches conducted as an outreach on Sundays. They invited people to come on a bus for a meal and a short Bible message and they would bring them back to the city at such and such a time. Lonely people from all walks of life, went for something to fill their time and for a free meal. Some found the Lord.

One of the leaders of the children's camps invited several of the younger men to a practical teaching and instructional camp over Easter. There were about twenty of us there, and we were learning how to lead a service, how to speak and give testimonies and stuff like that. In those days leading a service comprised mostly conducting singing and getting the best vocals from the congregation, as your personality and skill allowed.

I was one of the youngest and it was interesting to watch the guys from the larger city churches strutting their stuff. Guitars were just starting to be used among the youth in singing, but bands were growing in popularity for youth groups in churches. The leader beat time with his arms to the music. I was never able to master any of this, but some people used it for really good effect. I would have loved to have been taught about spiritual gifts and how to use them. I was about thirty-five before the full impact of Paul's teaching became a reality for me. These formative years helped me immensely to know God's peace in my life and His encouragement, as I yielded my life more and more to Him.

In February 1959 I went to the Melbourne Myer Music Bowl to hear Billy Graham who had come from the USA for a crusade. I came down on the morning train from Rosedale and arrived at the Music Bowl in plenty of time. As I was early, I got a good seat inside the covered area, but I also watched the set up and rehearsal of the choir and other performers. I'm not sure what day of the week it was but people were arriving from about 3pm for the start at seven o'clock. It was a lovely warm day and, in the evening the entire outside hillside was wall to wall with people sitting on the grass. I had never witnessed anything like it before.

The singing was stunning. Cliff Barrow led the service and community singing, George Bev Shea sang some solos with the choir as background, and Billy Graham preached. At the end there was the hymn, 'Just as I am', and people started coming from all areas of the crowd to make their commitments to the Lord. This was an inspiring experience I will never forget. I caught the train back to Rosedale the next morning.

In the Nambrok district, three men made commitments to the Lord. One was the husband of Doris Duke who attended the small church that was started in my parent's home some months before. His name was Jack Duke. The other two were sons of another lady who attended the church, David and Paul Smith. The lives of all three were completely changed, though on the journey each of them had struggles they had to face and overcome.

The Smith family became an integral part of the church. They owned the local post office and telephone exchange and when this was moved into the front room of a house next door, they offered the vacated rooms to be used for church meetings. It was ideal being next door and part of their property. With some renovation we were able – with a squeeze – to accommodate about thirty-five people. The church grew. To boost our Sunday School, and to reach out to people, Mrs Smith contacted a boy's orphanage about ten miles away at Kilmany and we went each Sunday with two or three cars to bring ten to fifteen boys for Sunday school and an afternoon tea. This lasted for about a year and we hope that something of the message of God's love was shown to the boys.

My parents entertained lots of visitors in our home. Missionaries who would come for shorter or longer stays, preachers or Bible teachers who came at least for a weekend, and of course Mr Toby in his Bible van. He always stayed at least a week. On his last visit to the farm, he encouraged me with his words of wisdom and blessing before he drove to Bruthen, for his next stop and visit. Two days later a phone call came through from Bruthen to tell us he had died peacefully in his sleep that night. His funeral was in Melbourne in his home church. This was the first funeral I attended, but I was so glad. It was inspiring to hear from so many people whose lives were changed by this gracious godly man in Victoria and Southern NSW. Two men told how Fred Toby was the catalyst for them planting churches that still flourish to this day. He was a keen cricketer and as a young man was in the NSW eleven, but decided to give his life to follow the Lord. What an example he was of God's love and grace.

By this time, I was preparing to go to Emmaus Bible School in Sydney with a view to getting a Biblical background before serving the Lord, wherever he directed me. Emmaus had commenced two years previously with six students. In February 1961 Kevin, a friend of mine, arranged to come to the farm for a night to take me with him to Emmaus. Another three friends were travelling with him. We were all going together sharing in the cost and in the driving of Kevin's VW Combie and a Triumph Herald. I sold my Plymouth to help pay for some of my fees. We took three days to get to our final destination via the Princes Highway and Canberra. I was glad to get to know these guys before I got to Emmaus. I don't remember much about the journey except I did enjoy Canberra. The war museum especially was a memorable visit for me. I loved the spacious layout of the city, and the view from a high hill was stunning.

Emmaus was a two-year course. Ian McDowell was the new principal. For our year there were thirty students in total and new buildings to house the influx were being sorted. They needed some work to complete, especially the toilets, showers, paths, drainage, outside painting and landscaping. So, while the main work was being finished there was lots of work around for us all when we had time between lectures.

On Sundays we went to a church of our choosing. The first one I went to was quite close to the school, but it was very conservative. Before very long those of us who went found other places where we felt more at home. In the second term I wanted to put my efforts into helping on a voluntary basis at the Lutanda Children's Home. I must have gone on public transport to get there and most of my time was helping in the large veggie garden which kept a good supply for the sixty or so children who were cared for in the centre.

Keith Young from Melbourne was caring for the boys in the home, but he was also the chief grounds person. We got to know each other quite well. On Sundays he called for me at Emmaus and took me in his little bubble car to a small country church about fifteen miles away. On occasions we went to a market gardener's place for lunch. He was growing cabbages at the time and invited me to go to the Sydney market at 4am one morning. I stayed with his family the night before and helped load the cabbages on his truck.

At 4am we set off for a most interesting experience of seeing how the fruit and vegetable market worked. Trucks were lined up loaded with produce in this huge barn-like structure. All the produce was packed in open boxes, and people would bid for the number of boxes of cabbages they wanted. When the highest bid was reached, all who wanted to buy cabbages could tell the auctioneer how many boxes they wanted. Most of the buyers were produce shop owners. We drove away after about four hours at the market when all the cabbages were sold.

For me, Sydney was a very difficult place to get my bearings. Apart from public transport I was mostly driven to places I needed to go. Frequently a team of us went to a church to take a service or into the city for an open-air meeting. Some of us went on Saturday and most Sunday nights for an hour to Pitt Street in Sydney Central. Ron Pearce drove his Holden ute. This was set up so the back cover lifted up from the left-hand side and became a backdrop for those singing or giving a testimony or preaching. I mostly operated a small loud speaker system from the open window of the passenger seat.

At the beginning of the second term a group of six of us met for prayer before going to the Open Air. We hadn't seen any real fruit for all the effort, so decided to ask the Lord for some real results. We started at ten people coming to a real relationship with the Lord over the following months, but in the end, we could only agree on three that were to be our target. When the time was up three people were saved and introduced to a church in the areas where they lived. But while our prayer was answered, we never again used that kind of prayer to see what God could do. I have often wondered why, but on reflection think it may have been because among us there were those who were not wholeheartedly committed to what the Lord could have done if our hearts were right with Him. However, I learned to trust and lean more on God's grace.

I disliked going into Sydney with its fast-paced bumper to bumper traffic, mingling with the crowd of drunks, druggies and prostitutes who wandered the streets looking for their next bit of excitement or pleasure. Some shouted abuse, but others stopped to listen. Some were regulars, but others were only passing through. All the time I was learning and growing in my journey with God, yet I felt so inadequate for the task. I hadn't mixed with crowds of people like this before.

In my first year I roomed with Robert Palmer from New Zealand. He came to do a one-year course only. He was a good soloist and gifted in a number of skills including a happy outgoing personality, but also prone to highs and lows emotionally. We were opposites in many ways. Apart from him falling head over heels in love with a girl he met from what is now Zimbabwe, he bought and sold two cars in the time he was at Emmaus. He married as soon as his time ended at Emmaus and moved back to New Zealand. My second year was with Ron Pearce from Melbourne. Ron was a plumber by trade and worked at keeping his business going while at Emmaus. Ron, like Robert, was also the life of the party type, with a great outgoing personality. I learned a lot from my time with both of them.

Our lecturers were a mixed bunch. We briefly touched on all the books of the Bible and several other subjects as well. Some lectures were quite boring, but most put in a depth of spiritual maturity which made the subjects come alive. Looking back now I wish I had put more effort into learning the Scriptures as there is such an untold worth of knowledge and understanding in them. I did gain an overall picture of how the Bible fits together and how to study it better, and that alone was worth the time spent. All that was aside from the different and interesting people I met and rubbed shoulders with.

Part of the course was a weekly lecture from someone in full time ministry either overseas or local. From this we gained a good understanding of lots of avenues of service. I wanted to know where and if God was leading me into missionary work and what were the options for me. It was more important for me to know God's prompting or guidance in my life than other factors. I was telling God in prayer that I was willing to go anywhere He called me. I waited, sometimes a little frustrated, knowing the Lord was leading other students who were already preparing to go to the Chad in Africa. They believed the Lord wanted them to go there. An Englishman came and spoke to us about the need in Brazil among the tribes of the Amazon basin, using a boat. I wondered if that was where I should go. I prayed and wrote to a missionary over there and got quite a negative reply.

In the meantime, on my way through Melbourne, I went to a missionary conference in Camberwell where Kevin Dyer from Tasmania spoke telling of the vast needs for teams to go to Asian cities with literature. He told of a ministry he commenced called Literature Crusade. In Australia and New Zealand, it was later known as Gospel Literature Outreach. Kevin spoke too of a boat ministry in Hong Kong, and the need for the Gospel among the many refugees who were fleeing from China's Communist dictator. Before the closing prayer, those who were willing to go where God called them, were asked to stand as an indication of their pledge to follow the Lord. I stood with knocking knees as I realised just some of what that meant in my life. I have never once regretted the decision. I look back now because then I was twenty years old. Fifty plus years have now passed. My journey of faith with God is still the most rewarding and unforgettable experience which I would not change for anything.

Back at Emmaus, I obtained the address of an English Brethren missionary in Hong Kong and wrote to him of my call from God to serve Him and my wish to know more about what was happening in Hong Kong. Raymond Guyatt wrote back a most encouraging letter, in which he told of Samuel as a boy, when God was speaking to him. Samuel thought it was Eli speaking. The Scripture Ray referred to in 1 Samuel 3:1-10 put the seal on the growing conviction in my mind that the Lord called me to Hong Kong. My assurance was that the Lord called me that day in the Missionary Conference in Camberwell, when Kevin Dyer spoke. I thanked the Lord and started taking the steps to make it happen and asking God to close the door for me if this was not His will. I asked the elders of the three local churches I was associated with to confirm with me and be prepared to commend me to the work, if they were satisfied that I should go. When they confirmed this, I met with an Advisory Council in Melbourne. This group of ten people were recognised as elders and could check on a person by asking the right questions. They were wanting to know if a candidate was a fit person to spiritually, mentally and physically represent their sending churches in a foreign land.

After having read the messages from the local church elders and asking me a whole range of questions, the Advisory Council verbally confirmed with me that I could start preparing to go to Hong Kong. They would advise my home churches and others who needed to know. They suggested that I should consider the linguistic course run by Wycliffe Bible Translators. I later met with some of them one more time for their prayer and encouragement, which was a great witness to me that this was the right path God wanted me to take.

My course finished at Emmaus in November 1962. My brother Jim met and became engaged to an ex-Emmaus student who also became the cook after her graduation. They were married in January 1963 in Moorabbin – a Melbourne suburb – and I was privileged to be best man. Jim and Betty returned to Emmaus for Jim to complete his second year.

I did apply for the Linguistics course and was accepted for the next intake in Brisbane for December 1963 to February 1964. Little did I know what was ahead of me before I was to embark for Hong Kong. After Emmaus I went back to Nambrok to help with things on the farm and take any odd jobs on offer. My older brother David was working for a contractor in cartage. He took a job spreading super phosphate but the guy who normally helped was off sick, so he asked me to assist. It meant driving a large truck, loading super bags off a train truck, and then driving the truck to a large farm and spreading the two loads of super off the trucks. It was a long hard day for me. I hadn't handled forty-pound bags of super for two years and was so unused to this heavy work. Neither had I driven a heavy vehicle like this before with eight forward gears. But I gained a few more dollars towards Hong Kong and the unknown future income.

My parents wanted an extra two rooms added to the sleep-out, so I offered my services. I thought I knew enough of the basics to get me through. Once I had figured it out it went together okay. I put into practice some of the lessons I learnt in woodworking classes at the Tech school. Those extra two rooms meant it was now a small flat. When later I brought my wife and our small daughter on leave from Hong Kong, we made good use of the flat.

Jack Duke from our church visited and asked if I would like to go with him for about three weeks to Western Australia. He had recently bought a new VW car and an aboriginal friend from NSW invited him to join in a trip around Australia. Jack told him he would go for three weeks. They were to meet in Port Augusta, South Australia. A couple of days later Jack picked me up very early in the morning. We started a journey I will never forget. The first night's stop was in a motel inside the South Australian border. After breakfast it was an early start and we drove through Adelaide to Port Augusta where I met Duncan Ferguson and his wife Blanche for the first time. They were a couple who were past the half-century in years and were working for the Lord amongst their own people, complementing each other so well in the process.

Duncan was born in Western NSW. His parents left the children to their own devices when they were growing up on an Aboriginal reserve. His education was totally neglected to the extent that he was unable to read and write. He became a Christian in his mid-twenties and left behind a life of drunkenness and violence. Often, he was taken in by the police, but his testimony was knowing Jesus brought a complete change for the better in his life. He taught himself how to read and write, earned enough money to support his young family and attended the local church regularly. His love for other people grew when he told about his newfound friendship with Jesus. Duncan and Blanche now gave their lives full time in ministry for the Lord.

It was quite a cultural shock for me because here I was at Umewarra Mission Station, surrounded by more dark people than there were white skins, for the first time in my life. However, after our three-day weekend stay with them, I came to appreciate something of their different culture and way of life which has been a continual learning curve to this day.

Ahead of us to Kalgoorlie was over two thousand miles on a road none of us had travelled before. The plan was to drive about three hundred and fifty miles per day and stop for the night. The Fergusons were driving an old International utility. The pet dog, which Duncan would throw in the back with all their gear each morning, was also going for the ride.

Along the main Adelaide to Perth road, we came to a sign which said 'Gravel road for the next one thousand five hundred miles'. There were several more signs warning of kangaroos, and recent carcass evidence of this too. The road was flat and uninteresting for most of those miles we travelled. There was only stunted tree growth and stubby bushes and grasses and little wildlife.

Before we crossed the border into West Australia, we went through a low bush area and as we rounded a bend in front of us was a group of about fifty aboriginal people with threadbare, filthy clothing waving us to stop. Little children whose bodies hadn't seen water flocked around all naked as we stepped from our vehicles. It was quite a shock for us to see them in the state they were, unwashed and half-starved. They gathered around the vehicles all talking excitedly in a language we didn't understand. At last Duncan talked with one who could speak English and said he would like to meet the elders in their camp. We followed them about a hundred yards under the stunted trees near to their makeshift dwellings. After some time of negotiation, through the interpreter, Duncan had permission to play his guitar and teach them a song. Blanche, with her beautiful voice, sang a song that they enjoyed. Duncan told them simply about Jesus and how he had turned his wayward life over to Him. He did that through the interpreter.

We left them with some food items and pictures for the children, but our hearts were saddened at their plight. In our prayer times together, Duncan's voice would often break as he mentioned before God, 'My poor people. Lord, some-how bring them into your love through Jesus.' Later we learned that the South Australian government was bringing them into a place where they would be housed and cared for. It is hard to say if this was the best answer for these nomadic people who always lived off the land. I wondered if this was the first time they heard of the name of Jesus. I hoped that it wouldn't be the last.

At about 4pm, each day we travelled, we would be looking for a campsite for the night. The first night we drove down a track and camped in a clearing in among a group of malley-scrub trees about two hundred yards off the road. We slept – under the stars on the ground – with air mattresses to keep us comfortable and the embers of our campfire to keep us warm. The Fergusons slept on a mattress in the back of their covered ute. We followed this process until we reached Kurrawang Mission near Kalgoorlie.

Breakfast was hot tea and porridge cooked over the campfire. We carried all the food and drink we needed, as well as extra fuel as supply stops were very infrequent, though we stopped at them for a break. One of the nicest stops overnight was when the road took a turn towards the coast and we could see the sea in the distance. We camped on a hill under the stars with a beautiful clear sky. It was a welcome relief after the dusty, potholed road we travelled on.

There was a downpour of rain the day before we were well inside the WA border. We came over a brow of a slight rise and saw what looked like a road block two or three miles further on. When we got there several trucks were bogged down to their axles. When the rain came one tried to get around the other, but with their heavy loads they were stuck fast. We later learned it would be a week or so before they would get out. There were six or seven of these situations before we eventually got back onto the tar seal. With careful driving our vehicles could get through, either between or right around the bogged trucks. This was unseasonal rain and in the low-lying areas of the road the heavy vehicles were caught. There were no bridges or culverts built in the roads in those days because the rain was so infrequent and the traffic didn't amount to much.

At last, we arrived at the Kurrawang turnoff. It was a mile on a dusty gravel road off the main highway to Kalgoorlie, which was fifteen miles further on. There were gums and low scrub along the sides of the road, but the dirt was all red. We crossed over the main rail line and the water pipe line and drove on past a high wire fenced orchard garden area to the main buildings of the mission among the now familiar cloud of dust and low gums.

The buildings consisted of five houses, a generator shed beside a garage, another building for kitchen dining and separate dormitory buildings for aboriginal girls and boys who were looked after at the mission. Further beyond these was a church building, and later I went to the huts beyond the church, which were for resident aboriginal couples or singles who lived on the site. There were about ten of these corrugated iron huts. Nothing was crowded as the whole property consisted of some three hundred acres of scrubby bush land.

We met with Will Sharpe and his wife. They were the founders of the mission and were an interesting and dedicated couple, but quite firm and sometimes dogmatic in their approach to some things. We were given a guesthouse for our stay and were to have our meals with the children. At that time there were about sixty girls and thirty boys who were sponsored by the government of the day to have this care and to be provided with an education. They were bussed into Kalgoorlie for their schooling. There were also about four girls and two boys who were not yet school age.

This was in the time in Australia's history of the so-called 'lost generation' of aboriginal children, when state governments deemed it necessary to take these children away from their parents and bring them up in 'proper' care with an education. Some of those poor kids were totally lost. They were in a culture they knew nothing of, wearing clothing and shoes which were not part of their bush way of life, among different children from different tribal and language groups, and having to live in a western house with sheets and blankets on their beds. Many of them could not speak much of the English language. No one tried to learn their culture or languages. Sorrow filled my heart at their plight.

Water at the mission was plentiful as they were tapped into the yard diameter pipeline that came over five hundred miles from Perth to Kalgoorlie. It was built when gold was discovered in Kalgoorlie and the chief architect of the build and design committed suicide a couple of days before the water flowed out at Kalgoorlie. He had expected the flow to be much quicker and because he thought it was not going to work, took his own life before the water flowed. It has been the lifeline for the city of Kalgoorlie, as it has a very low rainfall.

Kalgoorlie is an interesting place with large hotels on most corners of the main street. Low gums provide shade along the streets. When we drove a short distance east and north along the roads, as far as we could see were mountainous flat-topped slagheaps of grey waste from the mines. The slagheaps were not a pretty sight. There must be a very large cavernous hole underground.

We went for an overnight stay on the Cundalee Mission about three-hundred miles east of Kalgoorlie. The dirt road followed the main rail track east to Zanthus and then the road turned north for the last twenty miles. A Canadian couple commenced the mission about twenty years before with government permission, but they were unable to find water. With a rainfall averaging under ten inches per year, water was a major factor for life of plants, animals and people. The rain came over a three-month period only.

We had good fellowship with these dedicated folk, learning a great deal of the struggles and joys in the task God had called them to. I was impressed at their perseverance and faithfulness to the work among these primitive people, including the difficult job of translation of the New Testament into the native language of the area. This involved teaching them to read as well, so schooling was part of the work they did. Without computers or modern language tools, the translation alone was a lifetime job.

Before dark, we went to the aboriginal camp about a mile in the bush from where their mission buildings were. The missionary told us that things were tense among the people because one of the young men had raped an engaged teenage girl a week before. For punishment the tribal leaders decided that the offending youth would be held down and each man in the tribe was to spear him in his leg above the knee. He had almost died but was now recovering.

On each mia-mia – or bark lean-to shelter – were several spears and two or three boomerangs across the top of them. Most of the people were clothed in second hand western clothing if they wore any, but children ran around naked. The people were quite tall and thin. Food for them was quite scarce and mostly what they gathered or hunted.

The missionary told us how that often he would take two or three Aboriginal men as interpreters and go in his Jeep out into the desert looking for small groups of people who didn't have contact with Europeans. When they did find any, they would invite them back to the reserve where the mission was. Here they could live on the large Cundalee Reserve if they wanted to and have more plentiful food than was available in the desert area where they wandered. Two or three weeks later the small group would arrive having followed the vehicle tracks to the mission. Usually after they recovered in health with better nutrition they would go 'walkabout' again but now there was somewhere they could return to if the need arose.

In Australia there are numbers of small tribal groups of between fifty and two hundred people. They have different languages, though some of them can understand their neighbour's languages. This was an extremely primitive and poor people by our standards, though they have existed this way since birth and, just like me, they were known by God when He fashioned all their bones and sinews together in their mother's womb. It was a privilege and so interesting for me to be there.

A few short days later we were on our journey back to Victoria. Early one morning we said our farewells. The Fergusons stayed on for a few more days and then continued their journey to Perth and to isolated aboriginal settlements up the west coast and north to Darwin. From there across to the East and back to Brewarina in Western NSW where they lived.

Without the slow pace of the Fergusons, Jack drove the little beetle as fast as the roads allowed to get back as quickly as he could. We stopped only for food, petrol and probably three night's rest. I was amazed at how he could negotiate a group of potholes across the road width and catch just the most-shallow or miss them all. Jack was a driver of army trucks in the war in desert areas across the top of Africa. He was an excellent driver.

The roads were dryer and the bogged trucks were all gone. On our last day on the dirt road rain clouds were banking up behind us. That day Jack drove six-hundred miles on dirt roads before we were back on the tar seal. Two tired guys stopped in a dirty little grey beetle at the first motel we came to. When we arrived home, Jack took his car in for a ten-thousand-mile service. The garage folk thought this was a fifty-thousand miles service because the car was so worn on the tyres, bearings, steering and the underneath battering it had sustained from flying stones.

I had only been home about two weeks when I got a phone call from Mr Sharpe at Kurrawang asking me if I could go back to help them out until October because Leon Kessel, who was caring for the boys, needed to take time away because of illness. My first reaction was to say no, knowing that a trip back to Kurrawang wouldn't enable me to replenish the funds I was hoping to earn over the next three or four months. I needed a couple of days to pray about it. I promised to let him know after two days. The Lord assured me during the two days that He was quite able to supply all my needs and care for me too. I rang and told Mr Sharpe I was booked on the overland train to Kalgoorlie at such and such a day and time. I'm not sure if he offered to pay the fare, but my living expenses were all taken care of by the mission during my time there.

This time it took about a seventy-hour train ride with changes in Melbourne and Adelaide. I was able to book a sleeping berth and enjoy a half-round viewing lounge at the back of the train from

Adelaide. Not that there was much to see after we left Port Augusta except back down the straight track for miles and miles of bare barren country before the horizon dipped with the train-track until they appeared to be part of the vivid blue sky. We made several stops along the journey but only to refuel and let off passengers or most likely railway workers because after Port Augusta there were only a few houses and sheds at the stops I saw. No trees, just wind-swept tussock and stones for as far as I could see. As we closed in on Kalgoorlie, more trees and taller grasses were on both sides of the tracks. I was about 'trained-out' when at last I arrived at last. Mr Sharpe was waiting on the platform for me.

I soon settled into a routine. Instead of sleeping in the guest house I had a small room to myself in the five bedrooms where the thirty boys were accommodated in bunk beds. We all ate our meals together in a large dining room next to the girls' home. There were two single ladies who supervised some teenage girls who had left school and were in preparation for going into the work force.

The first week I was given a general rundown of my duties by Leon Kessel who had been at the mission for several years. He was married with four young boys. The oldest was about eight. Leon introduced me to all the people on the compound and took me when he went to visit the people living in their corrugated iron huts. I was responsible for the diesel generator that supplied power for all the buildings, the garden and the boys. Leon and his family left at the end of one week.

The time at Kurrawang was an excellent experience for me. The garden always needed working on. I learned how to prune grapes, and much good food was produced in the gardens which was all used in the kitchen. The best times I spent with the boys was when I could go in the bush walking with them and getting them to teach me some of the bush-craft they knew. This was like second nature to them. Some of the boys showed me the different track marks of the kangaroos, lizards, snakes, ants and small rodents. They became quite animated, and some would even get so excited they would speak in their mother tongue. I was able to learn a few phrases from them. Two of the older boys thought they knew if the footprints the animals left were fresh or not. One day we tried to work out how far the ants went for their food, but there were several different species and streams of thousands of them going across the red dirt in different directions. We soon gave up.

Getting the boys to bed at night was the same kind of problem my parents went through. The younger ones wanted to be up late like their older brothers. But what saddened me most was when Mr or Mrs Sharpe would tell me the sad stories of how the boys came to be at the mission. It was often through the death of a mother or father or both parents, or when all the food money was spent on alcohol and the children were left to starve. These were experiences I had not gone through in my childhood. I was so grateful to the Lord for my Christian parents and upbringing.

When the adults accepted me better, they taught me how to 'cook' and butcher a small kangaroo ready for their type of eating. Meat in their lives is the main staple and they always hunger after it. This roo was put whole on the fire by their camp. All his hair singed off while he was turned over in the hot coals several times. When they deemed he was cooked enough – or they were too hungry or impatient to wait longer – the roo was dragged out of the hot embers and hacked into chunks. These chucks, of blood oozing meat, were handed around with much joy to extended waiting hands, stuffed into their mouths and swallowed, without much digestion taking place.

Before the roo was taken from the embers a lady holding a stick over the fire took it out and on the end was quite a large scorched blue tongued lizard. She pulled the white flesh apart, found the blood oozing liver and offered it as a delicacy for me to eat. I'm not sure if I offended them by not eating, but it was too much for my delicate stomach to handle. She swallowed it with relish. Next day several of them were at the mission to see the nurse for medicine to help their aching stomachs. Maybe I would have been in the queue too if I indulged in some of their uncooked meat.

Each Aboriginal adult was given a small weekly government handout of money at the mission. Tuesday was their day to go to town. Some came back in the evening totally drunk. One elderly man came back and stepped out of the taxi with an immaculate white suit, new shoes and a red tie. It looked stunning against his dark skin. Three days later I saw him again, but now his shoes were missing, and the suit was covered with red dirt. He lived in his clothes for those three days and nights while sitting or lying on the red dirt around the camp fires. He was filthy. I'm not sure when he changed his clothes but I didn't see him in his new clothes again.

I learned that aboriginal people who dedicate their lives to God have insight and understanding of the Bible and the things of God equal to and sometimes beyond that of a lot of educated European Christians. Along with this, I also learned that 'missionaries' can become quite odd and sometimes isolate themselves into their own little world. This was a lesson I had to learn. Anything that would take away God's place in my heart would make me unproductive in my spiritual life and walk with Him.

The people of Kurrawang were invited north to an annual convention at a United Aboriginal Mission at Mt Margaret about two-hundred miles north. We travelled through Menzies, Leonora, and then east to Mt Margaret. Mrs Sharpe drove one vehicle and I drove the old International small bus. The younger children and some of the others stayed behind but both vehicles were filled with people and supplies for the two-night stay.

My memories of the journey are limited to a few main facts.

The road beyond Kalgoorlie was a seldom-used gravel, sandy, dusty, narrow track. There were a few wider places for passing or parking if we needed to. It was scrubby, bush-lined for some of the way. At other times we would come out to clearer areas of vistas filled with wildflowers as far as I could see. Sometimes brilliant red Stuart pea covered the whole landscape, but then over another rise, yellows or blues and often mixtures of beauty with all three colours present. It really was spectacular. This was God's special garden for me. It rained a few weeks before we made the journey, but as we got further north there no sign of any rain and the earth took on the familiar red dirt of that part of the land. The return journey I tried to take a little slower to take it all in. I have no memory of where or what we ate, where we slept, but only of me trying to catch up on some sleep if the opportunity arose, as this time my main responsibility was driving the vehicle both ways. But I do remember three fascinating Bible teaching sessions by an elderly aboriginal pastor. His subjects were Ebed-melech, an Ethiopian who saved Jeremiah from death when he was put down an empty pit in chapter thirty-eight of Jeremiah, Simeon who carried Jesus' cross, and of the Ethiopian who Philip pointed to Jesus in Acts chapter eight.

A friend of the mission visited from Perth and I was offered three days to return with him and his wife for a break from my duties. I gladly accepted, as I hadn't seen Perth before. This man was doing Gideon work one day while I was staying in their home. I was able to accompany him as we drove south of Perth for about three hours visiting schools where we distributed New Testaments to the school children. This had been previously arranged. On the return journey we stopped at a Nestlé's dairy factory and joined a guest touring party watching how they made condensed milk. I went with them also to their church in Perth and they drove me around to see some of the city highlights. Perth is a beautiful city on the Swan River.

It seemed very isolated from the rest of Australia or did at that time because air travel was not so efficient and the road across the Nullabor to Adelaide was so dusty and difficult. I travelled back to Kurrawang by bus which was a good journey too.

Just before I left Kurrawang, my replacement came in the form of John and Alison Salisbury and their two small boys. John had been in the airforce when I first knew him and he helped at the initial Tidal River camps we ran together with Alex Ronalds. It was a few years since I met him and we enjoyed each other's company for those few days.

The time at Kurrawang was an important part of my journey of faith, though at times there were frustrations and difficulties. There were some very committed people, Aboriginal and missionaries, who had dedicated their lives to serve among these people. Some I will never forget. I also realised what a vast empty country the land of my birth is, but here I was preparing to go to a small British enclave with a population then of about 3.5 million with lots of refugees risking their lives to get to the freedom of Hong Kong.

I don't have any recollection of my train journey back to Nambrok, but I suspect I tried to catch up on sleep as best I could on a noisy moving train. My reflection was of the whole experience of my life so far and especially my experience at Kurrawang. God had opened the path for me, provided my every need and protected me. I couldn't thank Him enough. It was the middle of October of 1963, and in the middle of November I would be preparing to go to Brisbane for the Wycliffe Summer School of Linguistics which was three months duration. I had applied for the course several months previously.

The Halls of Residence where we stayed at the Brisbane University were first class accommodation with all meals provided. The studies involved lectures in anthropology, phonetics, grammar, syntax and such. After five weeks, we took morning sessions in small groups with a foreign language speaker. I was in a group with a proud Muslim Urdu speaker from Pakistan. He soon let us know that his language, religion and culture was far superior to the Christian way of life. However, I started to grasp some of the difficulty of hearing the sound of another language.

The first six weeks would have been enough for what I wanted because the next weeks were mainly for those who wanted to get into the technical stuff of translation work. Many of those students were going into small tribal areas to do Bible translation. These were special training days. I learnt heaps on the course and later as I was learning Cantonese in Hong Kong, I was so glad for the introduction to language learning.

For some time, I was corresponding with a missionary in Hong Kong, but I got a letter from Bill Decker – one of the other missionaries – who asked if it would be feasible for him to come to Australia during the school holidays in Hong Kong. This was June and July and he was expecting to come for six weeks and travel around speaking to churches. His plan was that I would arrange meetings, travel with him and organise the arrangements. The Advisory Council thought it was a good plan as it would help me become known in Brethren circles before I left for Hong Kong.

It was not possible in six weeks to go throughout Australia, but together we made plans to visit Sydney, Brisbane, Melbourne, Tasmania, and Adelaide. Bill would go on to Perth himself and then to Hong Kong from there. There were designated people in each area who would arrange the meetings and accommodation when they were given the dates, so I contacted these people, who did an excellent job.

I met Bill in the Sydney airport very early on a cold June morning. We had meetings most evenings, others during the day, and we took in a few sights. We went to Emmaus and Bill spoke to the students there. Bill told how he and Viola, his wife, went to China in 1949 with a boat mission to Canton. Because of the Communist takeover in China, they were soon displaced to Hong Kong. Now, some fifteen years later, he was associated with the Brethren. He retained an interest in boats and boat people, but his main emphasis was in 'Roof Top Schools'. With the multitude number of refugees fleeing China to Hong Kong, a number of mission agencies and non-religious groups asked the government if they could use the rooftops of the buildings for schools for the refugee children. The Communists got in the act too.

The schools consisted of four classrooms, each holding about forty children. The classrooms were on the roofs of each of the seven-storey rough concrete buildings. They were seventy yards long by twelve yards wide, with stairs at each end. Communal toilets were in the centre of each floor. A five-foot wide walkway round each floor provided access to each twelve by twelve-foot room, with a door and window onto the walkway. Families of up to ten people lived in these crowded housing estates. The only redeeming feature was that there was more security for the people than in the make-shift squatter huts from which they came. Each building housed about two-thousand people. The school playground was the concrete roof, with a six-foot high fence around the perimeter.

This was a significant ministry Bill took in hand and there was evident fruit for all his efforts, as at that time there was practically a free hand for those who ran the schools to use them for extra-curricular activities on holidays or at weekends. Two sessions of school each day meant twice the numbers of children got a basic education. There was always a full roll and students paid fees, though many were sponsored from overseas. By the time I arrived in Hong Kong, Bill was responsible for five of these schools. Bible lessons were taught daily as part of the curriculum in the Christian schools.

Bill owned a boat in Hong Kong and employed a local Chinese boatman. In Australia he spoke of these two aspects of work he was involved in and spoke briefly of the other ministries the Brethren missionaries were doing.

We flew to the main cities because our time was short. We went to Brisbane, to Melbourne and out to Gippsland, across to Tasmania and then to Adelaide. I was getting to know Bill and even though I boarded with him in Hong Kong for more than a year, I never did fully understand this driven man.

I left Bill in Adelaide and he flew on to Perth for his final few days in Australia and then took a flight back to Hong Kong. I returned back to the farm and finished up the final preparations for my departure – health check, injections for several diseases, visiting relatives and friends I wouldn't be seeing for a few years and putting together the stuff I was taking with me. There was a combined farewell from the three commending churches, family and friends. Some couldn't really understand why I was leaving Australia to go to an unknown future in Hong Kong. However, I knew of God's call in my life to try as much as I could to live to please Him wherever He was leading me. Many from way back in Biblical times had shown the way in this. I have no regrets.

Top: Knowles Ancestors. Back row, left to right: Frank, George, Duncan, Agnes, Bill, Henry. Front row: Jim, Septimus, Great-Great-Grandma Helen, Great-Great-Grandpa James (the original convict), Great-Grandpa John (Jack), c.1895.
Bottom: Grandma Ethel Knowles, Grandad James Knowles, c.1950.

Top: Whitley Family. Left to Right: Harry, Marian, Grandma Clare, Geoff, Claire, Grandpa John, Ella (mother), Devonport, 1923. Bottom: Graeme, me, David, Neerim South, 1946.

*Top: Knowles Family. Left to right: Jim, Pete, Graeme,
Mother (Ella), Malcolm, Father (Percy), me, David.
Bottom: Me with my pet lamb (Lambie), Willung, 1950.*

Top: At Willung. Left to right: Me, Jim, Pete, Mother (Ella), David, Graeme, Malcolm, 1955. Bottom: At Kurrawang Mission with the boys I looked after, 1963.

Top: The Brown Family. Back row: Solway and Joy.
Front, left to right: Croydon, Janice, Maurice, Lesley, c.1949.
Bottom: Lesley on the eve of departing NZ for Hong Kong, 1966.

Top: Our wedding in Hong Kong, 1967. Bottom: Chung Tai Uk, the village near Shatin where we had a church, 1968.

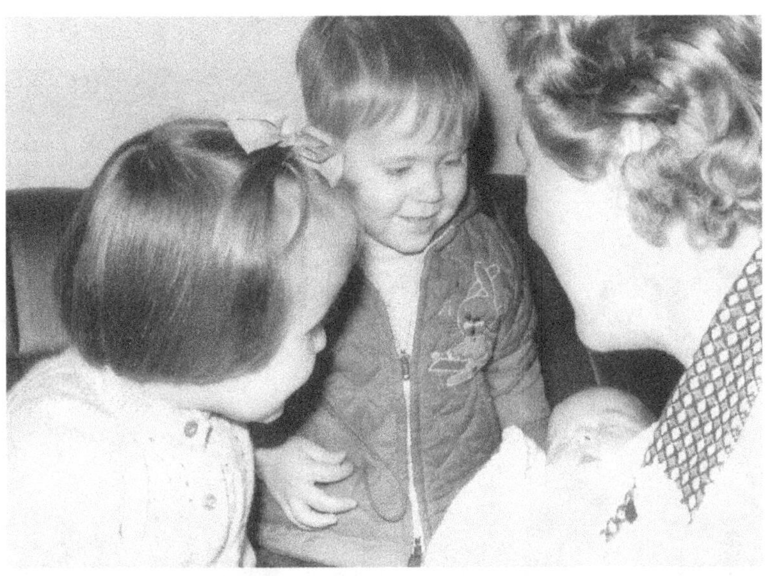

Top: Rosemary, Richard and Lesley (holding Christine and bringing her home for the first time), January 1973.
Bottom: Back in New Zealand. Richard, me, Christine, Lesley, Rosemary, 1973.

Some time later… Christine, me, Lesley, Richard, Rosemary.

CHAPTER 5

The P&O liner *Oronsay* left from Melbourne at 6pm on the 4th of October 1964 bound for Sydney, Manila and Hong Kong. There were several family and friends to see me off. With the streamers, waving, and slow progress of the ship moving away from the wharf, the process takes quite some time until the ship turns to head away.

I was sharing a four-berth cabin with two other guys about my own age. One was Irish out for a good time and the other was on this cruise as part of his annual holiday. We were all on different meal times, so we saw very little of each other. Their interests were the girls, the nightlife and the booze, none of which had any attraction for me.

At Sydney there was a three-day stop over. I previously arranged to fly to Port Macquarie north of Sydney to see my friends Jack and Doris Duke. They had sold their Nambrok farm and bought rental holiday flats at this seaside resort. It was so good to see them again. We did a lot of talking and catching up in between cleaning a couple of their flats, early morning walks on the beach looking for discarded refundable throw away drink bottles, and a couple of swims in the cool surf.

One day while swimming alone I got caught in a rip and carried outside the flag area. It wasn't much fun out in the deep stuff and I knew to keep calm. 'Lord, help me' was my prayer and a surfer on a long board was soon alongside me and telling me to hang on to his board. He signalled to the lifeguards and took me to shallow water where, shaking and spluttering, I was able to walk back to shore. The waiting angry lifeguard questioned me on why I went outside the flagged area. I told how I was caught in a rip. Did God send the surfer to pick me up? There was no one in view for me before he came. God's protection for us is quite special, but I hope I have never deliberately put myself in danger.

Sailing out of Sydney Harbour was quite spectacular. Once this long part of the voyage began it was good to get into the regular pattern of the ship's timetable. The food and cabin service on board was really good, and I enjoyed sailing inside the Barrier Reef for a good part of the journey up the Queensland coast. It was on that part of the voyage that I met and subsequently spent a lot of time with a retired man from Canada. His wife had died a year or so before and his two daughters in Vancouver persuaded him to go on this world cruise. Mr Harris had spent time visiting relatives in England, sailed through the Suez Canal to India then Perth and round the lower part of Australia. By this time, he was quite anxious to be back home again. There was still Manila, Hong Kong, and Japan to go before he reached Vancouver.

Mr Harris was a humble Christian gentleman. We shared our lives and some of our experiences together and it was good fellowship for us both. In Manila, where we stopped for a day in port, he helped me decide what to do. In each place where the ship anchored he went to the nearest bus depot and caught a bus that would take him far enough to see some sights, but close enough to get back to the ship before it sailed.

After parting with a few pesos for the fare, we boarded a colourful 'Jeepney'. This was an old wooden framed square bus which could seat about thirty people on wooden slatted seats. It was left hand drive, like all the vehicles in the Philippines. The driver couldn't speak English but was told to take us and bring us back.

We had no map and no idea really where we were going. This was my first introduction to an Asian country. All the traffic seemed to be heading the wrong way.

Manila itself was a busy bustling metropolis, but it wasn't very long before we were out of the city and passing through the countryside with high volcanic mountains. Everything was green and tropical. Bananas, coconut palms, rice paddies and market gardens of various crops looked luxuriant. Some were ploughing with rotary hoes, but most were using water buffalo for their power. The houses were often made from bamboo with rusty iron roofs, though there were many also in concrete blocks with iron roofs. Passengers were picked up and dropped off at various places along the way. Some bought local produce from the markets which included live chickens, ducks and baskets with all sorts of stuff like fruit and vegetables. There were children in school uniforms and others in the poorer villages with bare feet and tattered clothes. We saw the whole cycle of poverty and riches with the different styles of housing and way of life.

The road was busy with lots of dirty smoky trucks, buses, taxies, motor cycles, bikes and handcarts, vying for positions on the available space. The driver only knew one speed, and I was amazed at how close we went to all oncoming traffic on the narrow tar seal. Many times we were only three or four inches apart with both travelling in opposite directions at quite high speed on the open road. At first it was scary, but after a while I realised that I was in God's hands and that these drivers were quite skilled at what they were doing.

At last we came to the destination where we got out. It was at a port inlet on the other side of the island, or so it seemed to us. We were able to buy some fruit and juice for sustenance and go for a walk around the waterfront. There were several smaller coastal trader boats tied up at the wharf. All the loading and unloading was done by hand, with lots of slow-moving sweating bodies. This was the Philippines with its hot tropical climate and high humidity.

On our return the bus was loaded with crates of beer bottles from floor to ceiling except for the first four rows of seats in the front. We were surprised too, that there were no ropes to stop them moving forward if we needed to brake suddenly. We chose seats close to the door. The return journey had far less stops because there was no room for more passengers. The speed was the same and the old Jeepney leaned too far to the left or right around corners for my total peace of mind. We heaved a sigh of relief when we arrived back at the depot in good time for a shower and another shipboard lavish dinner just as the ship left for my last port, Hong Kong.

I was up early and out on deck at first light to see us coming closer into Victoria Harbour, Hong Kong. All my bags were packed and I rushed breakfast to get back on deck so I could get a good view of us tying up at this busy port. What a sight. The tall buildings on Hong Kong Island seemed to stand precariously close together without room for any more. Our ship turned to head into the wharf at Kowloon, while the whole harbour seemed alive with cargo ships, many smaller boats and Chinese junks jostling for their share of the water. Crowded passenger ferries were toing and froing across the harbour. Quite close to our ship were a number of small sampans – a small runabout boat – with four or five people in each. Standing in the rear of the sampan was a lady who was in control of the boat. She could twist the oar from side to side to make it go faster or stop. Somehow it looked so easy. Any children in these boats were shouting out to the ship's passengers to throw them coins. Some held nets on sticks to catch the coins, but if they missed the kids would dive in and mostly come up with the coin in their hand. We came quite close to a large Chinese junk in full sail as it made its way through the harbour. In cages at the back were several hens or chickens you could see. I later learned that these vessels also carried ducks, a couple of suckling pigs, some dogs, cats tethered on a string, and at least an extended family of twenty or so people, along with cockroaches, mice and rats. They carried cargo to make a living. During my time, illicit human cargo was sometimes found aboard these vessels with many people trying to escape from China to their freedom.

Small boats were getting closer and closer to the ship as it was slowly tugged into position. These had a contract to paint the ship above waterline on the outside before it left in two days. Probably ten of these positioned themselves with long poles on rollers ready to paint their section of the side of the ship. Some started as soon as we tied up with their small craft bobbing around in the wash of all the traffic on the water close by.

It took me some time to get used to all the crowds of people everywhere. I was unused to hustling my way through the overcrowded streets, squeezing my way on and off buses. Often, I boarded buses where the doors couldn't close because of so many people squashed inside. My time in Hong Kong taught me a lot about living in a different culture and about people of other races, and about how God works in our lives, or not if we don't walk with Him. I made lots of mistakes, but most important was the lesson I was learning to trust God more for all my daily needs. It's a lesson I am still learning as I get older, but I know there is no better path of life for me.

I boarded with Bill Decker for the first fifteen months of my time. He owned a two-bedroom flat on the tenth floor of an apartment building in Waterloo Road, Kowloon. Viola – Bill's wife – was in the States for most of the time while I was with them, but soon after she returned, I shared space with John Short in the YMCA by the Star ferry in Kowloon.

I learnt Cantonese with a private tutor. He was a good teacher and came to the house for three sessions in the mornings, five days a week. It took quite a while to grasp the basics of this tonal language in which one sound could have nine different meanings if spoken on a different level. I learnt to recognise and write Chinese characters as each one represents a single word. My teacher taught me the old script. In China at that time a simplified script was just starting to be used, but in Hong Kong its use was very limited. There are forty thousand characters in Chinese, and they can have up to fourteen strokes each as they are written. In learning the written form, I wrote the strokes in order and learnt them by repetition. I started with an inch square graph book and would fill a couple of pages with one character before I fully caught on. That's what the kindergarten kids were doing in their classes too. Really good scholars – I was told – could recognise about twenty thousand characters. In my time I could recognise about fifteen hundred and that was enough to read parts of the Bible. To read a newspaper you needed about five thousand. Each character is a different word. There is no alphabet like it in the English language.

On arrival in Hong Kong I became associated with an English-speaking Brethren church that had premises in Kowloon. People were always coming and going, but it met my needs while I was studying the language and settling to the way of life. However, during this time I was encouraged by the other missionaries to get involved in the Chinese Church at Chuk Yuen. This was where the Peace Clinic was located.

I attended on several occasions, but it didn't seem right in some aspects. About one hundred people attended regularly, but it was largely run by the missionaries and on their terms. It was easy to figure out that some of the people attending came because they were in the employ of the missionaries, though a good number of them were very genuine in their faith. Sometimes the Cantonese preaching was interpreted into another Chinese dialect. It was not a live active church, bubbling over with joy like it should have been. I never did feel at home in that church.

John Short was loosely associated with the group at that stage. John was an Australian from Adelaide who was a new Christian. He was associated with the YMCA in Adelaide and it was there that he become a Christian a year before he left for Hong Kong. He felt God's call on his life to give himself in service for God and landed in Hong Kong six months before me without any real support base. He rented a room in the YMCA by the Star Ferry terminal in Kowloon. John soon became involved in leading a couple of youth programmes there. By profession he was a dental technician, so he volunteered some time helping at the Peace Clinic. He did some dentistry work for a while, but because he was not registered, he ceased that work.

John and I became good friends and when my time was up at the Decker's, I moved to the YMCA and he and I shared a large room together. This saved both of us some cash. John was an intense person, yet to find his Christian roots. Because he was a new Christian, he was still learning the Scriptures and some of the more dogmatic people he encountered were quite out of character for him. While John was associated with some individuals of our Mission Group, he was never really part of us. More and more as time went by, he did his own thing and later became associated with a small more exclusive type group though he kept his ties with some of the open Brethren group as it suited him. During this time though, I was greatly impressed with his dedication to the ways and will of God for his life, and I think he and I were an encouragement and help to each other in our journey with God. John is a year or two older than me.

Among our group there were three families with young children. All were from England. Ray and Barbara Guyatt were in their early forties and had four daughters, Ruth about ten, Valerie eight,

Christine six and Mary about four. Ray was involved in Emmaus Bible Correspondence School, and the Scripture Gift Mission (SGM). Both of these were literature ministries. He commenced these in Hong Kong and they both proved to be fruitful ministries over the years.

Michael and Grace Browne had two children, Elizabeth eight and Andrew six. Michael was a Royal Marine with the British Army in Malaysia when he became a Christian. He was a brash person and the only grace he inherited was his wife who was very gracious towards all people, her husband included. I met with them often, as they were very hospitable. They went on a year's leave eight months after I arrived, and Jessie Scott and her two boys went at the same time to settle in England. All the children of school age went to English schools and this meant they used the same curriculum as they would have in the UK.

There were five single ladies connected with the group. Francis Wilks was about retirement age and her co-worker, Florence Hickson, was about forty years old. There was Faith Brunton, about thirty-five, and Ruth Whitehead from New Zealand, and Francis Hollingsworth from the UK. These latter two started the High Rock Christian School in Shatin. Ruth Whitehead's father was a New Zealand preacher/teacher and in this capacity had baptised my father in Kimberly, Tasmania in 1919.

Bill and Viola Decker were from the USA and were associated with a boat mission in 1948 in Southern China but left when the Communists took over. Bill found conflict difficult, so he tried to hide himself in a very busy life in school administration, fund raising and building of new schools which he did very well. In my opinion he offered little spiritually, though there were some quite able Chinese Bible teachers in the schools whose job was teaching Bible lessons. I learnt a lot by watching people's reactions to various situations.

Miss Wilkes and Florence Hickson lived at the Peace Clinic in an area of squatter shacks built on a hillside below Lion Rock mountain called Chuck Yuen. When I arrived, there was a church on the property which seated about one hundred and fifty people. The Guyatt house was there too.

Then I was added to this unique group of people. Most missionaries, unless they go out with the ability to work with a team, find enough excuses to hive off and do their own thing, believing God has called them to that purpose. In the experiences there were both good and not so good things I needed to take on board. It was a difficult place to live in many ways as a single person. However, I was aware of God's grace in my life and was thankful for every moment of His protection and guidance.

While learning the language I attended a small English-speaking church in Kowloon and, on occasion, a Cantonese service so I could hear the language. The English church was attended by several of our missionary group, a Chinese doctor and two of his doctor sons and their spouses, three or four expat business people, a young man from the British Army (married with a small family) and an Irish trainee police officer, about my age. Often there were USA or British sailors who met with us while in port. The Vietnam War was in full swing.

A British man named Roland Morrinson attended the church on occasions. He was married to a doctor whose parents were missionaries in Malaysia, and was a correspondent journalist. Roland sometimes preached at the church and some thought of him as an elder, but I never did get anything from his messages that touched my heart. He came across to me as someone whose message was from his intellect and not from time spent with God. On Sunday afternoons Roland led a Bible discussion in his home and I was persuaded to go on one occasion. The young Irish police trainee also came along. Before the discussion he was chatting with me about the centre where he was based and the temptation to have booze every day. He told how he was the only one out of all of them who was not into alcohol. Ian asked me to pray that he could resist the temptation, which for him was strong.

When the Bible discussion was completed Roland went to a cabinet and asked everyone what they would like to drink. There in the bar was a whole array of alcoholic drinks, which he duly started to dispense. There was juice available so Ian and I took that, but we were both embarrassed and I determined not to knowingly put a stumbling block in the way of a young Christian if I could avoid it in the future. In fairness to Roland, he was not privy to our discussion, but Ian didn't come back to our church. I learned many years later that Ian was still in Hong Kong and a Christian policeman in a high position in the force. That knowledge was an encouragement to me, because I knew that bribery was rife in the Police Force and Ian would have to fight that temptation too.

There are two other incidents I confronted in my single days that are worth a mention. Faith Brunton was not endowed with a lot of grace, charm or personality. She was a lady whose home church were opposed to her coming to Hong Kong, but she told the elders she was going anyway because the Lord had called her, so they relented and commended her. There was no place for her, but she was one of our group.

There was a typhoon in progress and people were asked to stay indoors as the winds were quite severe. I got a first-time phone call from Faith and she was in a panic because a window had broken in her flat and she couldn't get anyone to come and fix it. The time was after three in the afternoon. Reluctantly, I got on my motor bike and carefully rode through the rain and strong winds to her flat. As best I could I put a board over the window which didn't stop all the rain, and told her I couldn't fix it anyway. I turned to walk away and she stood in front of me and proposed. I was somewhat stunned, but clearly told her that I was not in the least bit interested and quickly departed. I told Viola Decker about the incident and she must have talked to Faith because there were no further problems with her. Not long after Faith returned to the UK. Soon after we heard she married a Chinese man and gave birth to a couple of children. They were not very old when Faith died.

On the opposite side of things there was a young Chinese student who visited at the YMCA sometimes for a meal or a cool drink on the roof garden. A couple of times John Short and I ate our meals with Ah Chun and heard his story. He said he was a refugee from a wealthy family in Shanghai. It was hard to know what was true of his story. We took the opportunity to tell him the story of Jesus and he appeared to want to know more. He invited me to a restaurant meal to which I went and then he asked me to his apartment. It was a dingy single little windowless room in Kowloon, on the seventh floor. It was furnished with a bed and a chest of drawers and two chairs. Ah Chun locked the door as we entered.

We sat down and he served tea which is the Chinese custom. For a few minutes he asked me about my story and I briefly told him about my childhood and youth. He then asked me if I wanted to play five hundred. I told him I had never played cards. 'I'll teach you,' he said. 'The loser of each game takes off one item of clothing each time he lost the game.'

I realised that Ah Chun was homosexual, and when I confronted him with this, he became quite angry. He said what he called himself, a poor refugee, trying to make a place in Hong Kong. He said, 'I paid for your meal before,' with a grudge in his voice. 'I just want you to be my friend.'

I quietly asked the Lord for his protection and to give me wisdom to get out of the situation. After the 'act' of anger and then sorrow, he at last saw that he had lost me and so unlocked the door and I departed, a little older and hopefully a little wiser.

When I told the YMCA manager, he was very angry and he told Ah Chun not to enter the premises again. As I write this I wonder if there could have been a different scenario for both the above incidents. Both situations needed the Joseph approach – as in the story with Potiphar's wife, he fled. *Thank you, Lord, for your help and protection for me.* I consider these were tests for me that would have wrecked my life's journey with God if I had walked the Tempter's road.

To get around the colony I purchased a small motor scooter, a Honda 50cc. It made such a difference in that I was able to go off the beaten track rather than on bus routes only. Often, I used to ride up into the hills above Kowloon. It was from here I could look down on the crowded city below, and if the weather was excessively hot at sea level it was always a couple of degrees cooler higher up the hills. With the bike I could also go on some unkept tracks and one of these led into a beautiful stand of bamboo. Bamboo growing by itself in the wild can be quite stunning if one goes in among the stalks. There are many shades and colours of different species. This stand was a lovely golden variety with thin stems up to one-inch across at the base. It was one of bamboo's smaller varieties.

One clear evening I rode up that track and stopped to take a photo of Hong Kong Island in the background with its towering buildings and backdrop of tall peaks, with Kowloon below in the foreground. I felt a sudden terrible loneliness. While I lived in a compact city with three and a half million people going about their stuff, and while I made friendships with others, I felt this total aloneness. For several minutes I sat down and wept. There were times when I missed family and friends in Australia, the wide-open spaces, the gum trees, birds, and even Vegemite, but it was not so overwhelming as this time.

When my emotions gave way to more rational thought, I felt

the ever-loving presence of the Lord. This too is hard to put into words, but it was as though He was saying again to me, 'I am with you, and I will never leave you. Don't be afraid. You are here for my purpose.' It was like a mountaintop experience for me. I thanked the Lord for showing me a small glimpse into the utter loneliness of the human spirit and for His peace and joy that I felt with His presence. Now whenever I think of the aloneness of Jesus in His trial of suffering for me, my small glimpse is nothing at all in comparison. And my joy of knowing that He cared for me then, is only a foretaste of the time when I will be in His presence forever. I also asked the Lord for a wife, someone who would be about the same spiritual level as me with a deep commitment and love for Him. Someone who would be a helper and share in the work of God, whatever He wanted us to do. God's peace swept over me, that peace the Bible talks about, 'Peace that passes all understanding.' It was so real I didn't need to ask again. I felt as if God had already answered.

Oh yes, I did visit the bamboo forest a couple more times after that. Once I saw a movement and it was a three-foot long thin green bamboo snake. He flicked his orange tongue at me, but he was far enough away from my space to do me any harm. He soon slithered off higher into the bamboo. I was more watchful in and among bamboo after that experience.

In time off in school holidays I would take the other missionary children for a walk up into the hills above Kowloon. Some of the younger ones were a bit of a handful, but mostly we had good times. They were not used to this kind of thing, but at least it gave their parents a break, and I liked getting away from the crowded streets especially in the early days when my Cantonese was in the first learning stages. Once we made it to the top of Lion Rock. Quite a climb.

My initial interest in Hong Kong was first raised by Kevin Dyer in Camberwell, Victoria when I heard him speak at a missionary convention. He told of this ministry among boat people that was not being done because of lack of personnel to do it. I lived about a year in the colony before the day came when we were to go to Lantau Island and preach to some village people there. Four of us, Bill Decker – the boat owner, Michael Brown, a Chinese preacher and me, went early to the mooring where the boat was tied up. There was a Chinese man who lived on the boat to care for it and he came in a little dinghy to the shore and rowed us out. Then we started the process of getting the boat ready. It was a Chinese-built boat, the shape of a small junk twenty feet long with a diesel inboard motor. Bill fussed around until he at last started the motor and slowly made our way out through the many family dwellings of different sized boats. We followed a channel that took us out past the entrance of the typhoon shelter to the open harbour. The typhoon shelter was a high stone wall built out into the harbour as a mooring place and shelter for hundreds of smaller boats.

Some of the larger vessels that sheltered there had chooks, ducks and even small pigs in cages. All had at least one mangy dog and probably several families of cockroaches that scuttled about especially after dark. Some of the children would go to and from school off the boats, as this was their home. It seemed a long slow chug-chug type voyage to the island as the boats top speed was six knots an hour. We had twenty miles to go. When hours later we arrived near a village we dropped anchor off shore and ate lunch before rowing ashore. There were barking dogs among the shy children who gathered to welcome the 'Gwai Lo' – foreign devils – to their part of the world.

This village was surrounded by rice paddies and vegetable gardens. Eventually we were invited into a small house and offered stale cookies and a cup of tea. Old stained cups were served with hot black tea and lots of sugar. We sat and were warmly welcomed to their village and the home. Through this time there was Chinese language chatter going on as to the purpose of the visit. We sipped some tea while time was requested to tell the children a Bible story. So we all went outside where the children gathered around and they were told a Bible story in their own language. The adults stood off at a distance, though some went back to their chores. There was a god-shelf in the house, so we knew they had no understanding of the true and living God.

We made our way to another village along the path. It was about a mile away over the hill and further up from the beach. All we were able to do was pass a few picture leaflets to a small group of children. The adults, very politely, made it clear that they didn't want us to talk to them. We left and made our way back to the boat. Now it was time to go back to Kowloon. A wind was getting up and the return journey was quite rough. It was late when we arrived back that evening. This was my first and last journey on the boat. I have even forgotten its name.

Soon after that journey I reflected long about the real value of the outing. Was this really why God brought me to Hong Kong or did He have some other purpose? Was there a better way to reach the people in the islands who mostly spoke a different Chinese dialect to the Cantonese I was learning? My answers soon came in the following ways. I was finding a lot of satisfaction in the work of Emmaus and Scripture Gift Mission. If I managed both they would be a full time occupation. However, there was another very logical cost-saving method to accomplish what we spent a whole day doing. The colony was blessed with an efficient ferry service. If one desired, one could go on the ferry in a third of the time it took us to Lantau and catch a return trip later in the day. Or stay for a few days and walk to the villages dotted around the coasts.

In Australia God focused my attention on Hong Kong by putting the need of a 'boat ministry' before me. Now that I was here, He was showing me quite clearly my purpose and the path I should go. I learned that day people are vitally important to God. I knew that in the literature ministries there was the prospect of reaching thousands of people with God's word. Of course, those island people were just as important to God too, but my focus now was what I believed was God's path for me. It certainly proved to be so in my life. *Thank you, Lord.*

Lesley Brown arrived in Hong Kong early in March 1966. She travelled from Auckland with the Guyatt family who were in New Zealand for a few months while Ray recuperated from illness. They arrived on the same P&O liner I had sailed on eighteen months previously. Lesley rented a room on the ladies' floor of the YMCA and soon settled into a routine with her language learning at an international school which took up her full time. It was an intensive course and she learned quickly.

Lesley was in Hong Kong three months before I invited her out. Our relationship grew and we were officially engaged on the last day of September 1966. It was a full moon and a beautiful clear evening and we stood together on the top deck of the newly built Ocean terminal overlooking the lights of Hong Kong Island across the water from Kowloon. Actually, it was also one of the Chinese festivals, but of course that was far from our minds. Now we were able to go places together and were company for each other and able to talk about our situations and relationships with our fellow workers. I learned about her family and the beautiful country she called home.

Among the missionary personal in the Brethren team, we clicked best with Ray and Barbara Guyatt and Ruth Whitehead and Francis Hollingsworth. Ruth was from New Zealand and the others were from the UK. Ray was responsible for both SGM and

Emmaus ministries and I became involved in these. I was left in charge of them while Ray and his family were in New Zealand from three months from Christmas 1965 – March 1966. However, before we married, Ray and Barbara and their family left for a position in Australia with SGM. They went in June 1967 so now I was in charge of the two ministries. There was something regular to put my mind to. Mostly I would do a morning in Emmaus and the afternoon in SGM.

About that time Lesley and I were giving more time to the children's and youth ministry at High Rock Christian School at Shatin. This was on weekends and during school holiday programmes. Francis Hollingsworth was the driving force behind the school. She had recently taken it over after an English lady who ran an orphanage was able to go back to England, taking the twenty or so Chinese orphan girls who remained with her. They were all granted British residency.

Francis and Ruth lived in a flat in the top floor of what was the old Shatin Police Station on top of the hill called High Rock. They invited us to go and live next door to them if we could fix up the other wing of the top floor for our accommodation. This we fixed before our wedding. We put in new steel-framed windows all around, a bathroom and kitchen, and divided off what was an open veranda to make another bedroom.

We walked up hill from the road about a hundred yards to the front gate. Up the path to six steps, which led to the front door. Ahead were another sixteen steps; a right turn at the top and four paces to the door into our flat where we entered into the lounge room. There was a ceiling fan in the centre of the lounge, and later we purchased an air conditioner for our bedroom. Water heating was with two instant gas heaters for kitchen and bathroom. I made a small table in the kitchen, but our main dining was in the lounge. All floors were concrete.

When we first started courting, Lesley and I were helping on Saturdays at Shatin where there was an afternoon youth group. This was a relaxed time for us and a good learning time too, both in making friends with the young people, and learning more about the culture and language.

Before we were married, some of Lesley's family arrived to be with us for the wedding and to have a couple of weeks holiday in Hong Kong. The first time I met them, Lesley's mum was quite sick and jaundiced because of one of the injections she got before leaving New Zealand. Lesley's sister Janice came as she was to be the bridesmaid. Lesley's eldest brother and his wife, Croydon and Margaret, were there too. Instead of coming, my parents had opted to send some money to help us get our home together. My brothers also contributed in this way and it was greatly appreciated as it enabled us to finish the house before the family arrived.

Here begins a brief history of the early Brown families who were pioneer boat builders. This is an extract from the journal of Lesley's great-great-grandfather, William Paine Brown, Master Mariner and Boat Builder of Te Wahapu, Bay of Islands, New Zealand.

The Family Bible records have the fact that I was born at Deal, Kent, England on the 17th of February 1815. After some preliminary instruction at home, I was sent to school at an early age, to Mr Claringbold, who conducted an education establishment for some of the Pilots and others, in the town of Deal. My father was a Pilot in Deal. At the age of twelve, I was taken from school and apprenticed to my uncle, a Boat Builder of Beach Street Deal with whom I remained until my sixteenth year. I was then expected to gain further knowledge of the business during my three years' experience as a carpenter's mate on board the Whale ship Pusey Hall *commanded by Captain Newby, a friend of my father.*

After six years aboard the whaling vessel, with a short time back in England to spend with his family, William found himself back in New Zealand waters in January 1836. There were many adventures as they sailed back and forth in the Pacific hunting whales for their oil. Further information can be gleaned from a copy of the journal he wrote in the book *Lanes & Browns of Early Northland*, pages 97 to 104. The book was compiled by Edith Lesley Grindall and Veda Joyce McKay for the 1985 Lane and Brown reunion.

The *Pusey Hall* lay at anchor off shore at Kororareka (later named Russell) in the Bay of Islands. William decided to leave the ship and go into hiding in Kawakawa because of trouble there was on board. He was at Kawakawa until the ship sailed and then made his way back to Kororareka where after a few weeks he took a job on a schooner called the *Columbine*. This was a vessel owned by the Church Missionary Society which took supplies to the different mission stations in parts of the North Island. They also carried mission personnel between the stations. There were no roads or railways in those days.

Three years passed and William signed off from his job on the mission ship. He met up with a former English friend, Mr Gardiner, and they bought three hundred acres of land at Te Wahapu, about three miles south of Kororareka. This land was suitable to start a boat building business which they set up in the early part of 1840. They built one house first and both lived in it until William found a wife. He wrote in his journal,

At this time there were only three white women living in the Colony who were unmarried and I was fortunate in winning one for my wife. We were married on December the ninth, 1842. Shortly afterwards, a family named Cairns came to live in a big house not far away and Gardiner found his wife in Miss Cairns, their eldest daughter. They were married during the year 1843. In 1850

> *Mr Gardiner died leaving a widow and two little daughters. By this time my family numbered four, two boys and two girls.*

William's wife Catherine, nee Reagley, was an Irish girl who came to New Zealand as a nurse maid for an English family. There were eight children born from 1842, Stephen, Jane, Kate, William Junior, Elizabeth, Emma Rose, Emma and Annie in 1861. However, not long after the birth of Annie, Catherine died from pneumonia, which was a result of her rounding up sheep during a storm in 1861. William and his family were devastated by the loss of their mother. William Junior was eleven when his mother died. Catherine's grave is at the back of St Paul's Church in Paihia. The family rowed across to St Paul's each Sunday. The children settled again to their lessons in the school room built on their property by their father. Other children also attended who were rowed to and from school. Mary Elizabeth Lane was the teacher, whose parents brought their nine living children from England, arriving in New Zealand in August 1860. Mary was the eldest of the family at age twenty when they arrived with timber to build a house on land at Kaeo. She was trained in England before coming to teach in New Zealand. One of her brothers was living on the Brown property and being apprenticed as a boat builder by William P. Brown.

Although there were twenty-five years difference in their ages, William decided to ask Mary to be his new wife as she already knew each of the other Brown children. So, on the 23rd of January 1862, they were married in the same church where Catherine was buried a few months before. The family grew from 1863 when Alfred was born, Herbert, Mary Louisa, Agnes, Gilbert, Winifred, Ethel, Edith till 1879 when Mary gave birth to a son who died soon after his birth. Mary Elizabeth was such a loving mother to all the children of both families and they always considered themselves as one family, never as two.

William Paine Brown witnessed much of New Zealand's early history. He witnessed Whaler's Port of Russell, participated in early missionary endeavours, lived through the history-making days of the British residency and the signing of the Treaty of Waitangi in 1840. He experienced the Maori Wars of 1845 to 1847 and pioneered ship building in the Bay of Islands. His first wife Catherine and the younger Mary Elizabeth, were both hardy, resourceful people, with the pioneering spirit which enabled them to leave the traditional ways of the Old Country and brave the unknown future halfway around the world. They proved themselves able to adjust to change while contributing their share to the development of the 'good land' in which they lived and successfully raised their large family. (Quote, Robert Bell)

In the year of 1870 two young men left the Bay of Islands in an open boat and pulled around the coast to the Whangaroa Harbour, a distance of about forty miles. They were determined to carve out a business for themselves on their own account. Both had served their apprenticeships with William Paine Brown in his ship yard at Te Wahapu, the Bay of Islands. The elder, Thomas Major Lane, was twenty-three and the younger, William Brown was twenty and the fourth son of W.P. Brown's first marriage to Catherine. They commenced the strong partnership of Lane and Brown which became known throughout New Zealand, Australia and the South Seas for its excellent ships.

The two men headed first for Kaeo where the Lane family from Gloucestershire had taken up land. It was there they built their first ship. They planned to run it between Whangaroa and Auckland to improve the poor existing communications. She was a schooner of seventy tons and forty-five feet long, clinker-built and proved to be both smart and successful. On one occasion she did the round trip in four and a half days while fully laden both ways.

Having a government grant of forty acres of land on the harbour at Totara North, the young men established themselves there. Thomas Lane married Margaret Hare in April 1872 and built a house overlooking the harbour and the new mill and yards. They had a family of six sons and three daughters. However, William Brown waited seven years before he married Fanny Laura Lane in March 1877, a younger sister of his step-mother, Mary Elizabeth. Fanny was twenty-one and William twenty-seven. Fanny loved children. This was one reason why they had a large family of seven sons and four daughters. They lived in a spacious house with a commanding view, on the property at Totara North.

The business Thomas and William commenced, eventually came to be regarded as the leading shipbuilding establishment in New Zealand with a covered space of fifteen thousand square feet, giving room to build up to three-hundred-and-fifty-tonne vessels. The firm's reputation extended far beyond New Zealand. They supplied vessels to Sydney and other parts of Australia, to the South Sea Islands and New Guinea. A fleet of fourteen pearling boats for James Clarke and Company on Thursday Island, who in a letter to the builders expressed in glowing terms their complete satisfaction with the faithful manner in which the contract had been executed. A further fleet of twelve Pearlers were built for Mr Cook of Cooktown. These Pearlers were twelve to fifteen tonnes and were delivered across the Tasman by the builders. For the first seven years of the partnership, the ships they built were only up to fifty tonnes, but in 1877 they increased the room to build the bigger vessels. Between 1870, when the partnership commenced and 1900, seventy ships were built by Lane and Brown of Totara North. Thomas Lane was in charge of the office and business side of the partnership while William Brown did the designing, moulding and supervision of building, until the sons of both families grew up and entered the business.

William Brown was considering what he should do to give his family a future. He and his wife decided to reluctantly move over to Northern Wairoa and set up a similar shipbuilding yard, naming it Brown & Sons, at Te Kopuru. They loaded one of the boats they had built, sailed around the top of the North Island and turned south to the Kaipara Harbour before coming to their new home at Te Kopuru. Eventually, six of William's seven sons were working in the business, Ray and Maurice were shipwrights, Clem and Archie were engineers, Frank was a painter and Syd, a blacksmith. In all, thirty men worked at the yard. The seventh son Edgar, operated a towing service on the Northern Wairoa River.

However, during their shift, at least one of his sons had to take his pony. This is what Clem wrote about his ride. Clement Solloway Brown became Lesley's grandfather.

Speaking of myself, I was only thirteen when my father William Brown of Lane and Brown of Totara North, dissolved the partnership and moved with his family to Te Kopuru, Northern Wairoa to make a fresh start with his seven sons. I had been to Prince Albert College for nine months and the shift put an end to that. I rode my little mare 'Bessie' from Kaeo to Hokaranui, the then rail terminus and the next day to Wangarei. After a day's spell, the next stage was to Paeroa via Waipu and finally to Mititai on the Northern Wairoa where my brother came with a launch and punt and picked me up with the gee-gee and delivered me to the new home in Te Kopuru.

I went to Aratapu High School for a while and then helped in the new firm of Brown & Sons. When I was seventeen, I got my heart's desire of becoming an engineer's apprentice with W O Ryan and Co behind the old railway wharf and next door to Logan Bros boat yard. Later we moved to Quay Street in Dargaville. It was in this period I got twelve weeks off to help with the lifting of the barque Wai-iti, that had capsized in the Wairoa River. Bye for now.

Over a period of some twenty years, Brown & Sons built one schooner, three scows, three steamers, four oil engine vessels, three large cattle barges, six lighters for carrying frozen meat from the works to overseas ships, as well as many small barges and launches. The mill at Te Kopuru suffered a disastrous fire in 1908. In addition to boat building, saw-milling and shipping kauri gum, they also built houses, wharfs, manufactured and installed windmills, water pumps and later milking machines with engines to drive them. Power didn't reach the region until 1936.

Clem S. Brown married Edith Franklin in 1910. Their five children were Solloway, born in 1911, Elizabeth 1913, Maxwell 1914, Lois 1916 and Owen was born in 1922. All the children had Franklin for their middle name. The boat building side of the business came to a halt because of Ray's retirement through sickness. He was the acting manager, and together with the effects of World War I, Clem and Archie decided to shift the engineering section to Dargaville. It was 1916, and Dargaville was the centre of commerce for the whole district. Four of the houses they had built in Te Kopuru, were barged to Dargaville where Clem and Archie moved with their young families. The arrival of the motorcar added a new side to their business. From the age of twenty-five Lesley's Grandpa Clem, was totally deaf. His children and grandchildren had to write, draw or sign with their hands in everything they wished to communicate with him. He was very observant and ran a successful business.

In 1937 Clem bought out Sigleys of Okaihau and shifted his family and engineering business to nearby Kaikohe, where Brown & Sons continued until Clem retired. His son Max continued with a chain saw motor-mower shop on the premises until the early 1970s when he sold the business and moved with his wife to Taupo. His sister Lois, Aunty Loie, started a very successful business in a wool shop in Kaikohe and took care of her mother until she died in

1960. Lois also sold her business in the early 1970s. She bought a wool shop in Taupo and all the while she cared for her elderly father Clem. I knew him in his later life and he impressed me as being a very godly person. Like his own father, Grandpa Clem continued to trust the Lord, until he was at last taken to be with the Him forever in 1974.

But I must get back to Lesley's parents. Solloway Franklin Brown and Joyce (nee Arthur) were married at Ellerslie in 1937. From the time their names were linked, they were known as Sol and Joy to their friends and extended family and Dad and Mum to their children. I will refer to them as Dad and Mum who, after their marriage, rented a house in Auckland for about a year while Dad continued to work for a clock maker. He took the job while studying for his accountancy papers and while he was boarding with one of his mother's relatives, the Franklins. Dad's family were at that time living in Dargaville and he told me he needed to take a steam ferry from Dargaville to Helensville and then get the train which took him to Auckland. Sometimes, while on the ferry going past the entrance to the Kaipara Harbour the sea would be very rough. The whole journey would take about five and a half hours, whereas today by road it takes about two and a half hours.

Mum was brought up at Ellerslie and she was the fourteenth and youngest in her family. Her father was a confectioner by trade, and came from England in the last part of the 1800s. Lesley didn't know much of her maternal grandparents or their family. Mum was not brought up with Christian parents and it wasn't until her fifteenth year that her older sister Lillian, led her to the Lord. Lillian witnessed to several other members of her family and they too came to know the Lord. Mum first met Dad at her home church, the Ellerslie Gospel Hall.

After their marriage they moved to Kaikohe so Dad could work in the family business again. They rented a farm house on the out-skirts of Kaikohe, six hours north of Auckland. Their first baby was a boy, Croydon, who was born at Rawene hospital which was about twenty-five miles over a rough, gravel, potholed road. It was February 1938 that Croydon came into the world. Lesley was added in May 1940. Mum was not prepared to go the distance to the Rawene hospital, so this was a home birth with a midwife present. Just as well, I was told, because Lesley hastened to be born and start this new phase of her life. Janice was born in June 1944, and Maurice in February 1946. Dad served time in the RNZAF, based in the Northland, but when the war ended, he was discharged and moved his family to Tauranga a few months after Maurice was born.

In Tauranga, Dad worked as the accountant for a garage and car sales business. They lived in a transit hut for two years, until they were allocated a house on the corner of Fifteenth Avenue and Cameron Road. The draughty, crowded hut was a difficult period for the young family and they were very glad of the shift. Dad and Mum became renters of their Housing Corporation home, which later they were able to purchase. When they reached school age, each of the children attended the Tauranga South Primary School.

On arrival in Tauranga, Dad and Mum attended the Brethren Church in Cameron Road. However, they moved churches when a new church was planted from Cameron Road to Greerton. That was in a new suburb about two miles from their home in the opposite direction to Cameron Road church. The Brown children sat in the front row of church with their parents. As a child Lesley was very well behaved. However, she did tell me of one incident when she was supposed to take a cod liver oil tablet each day. Sometime later her mother was doing some gardening outside her bedroom window where the horrible tablets had come to rest.

After Sunday school, when Lesley was about eleven years old, she told her parents she wanted to talk with Mr Edgar Smith who was her teacher. So, Lesley jumped on her bike and rode four miles and told him she wanted to give her life to Jesus. He was a very wise and godly man who pointed her to the Lord. From that day she determined in her heart to live to please the Lord Jesus and follow Him wherever He would lead her. She also enthusiastically helped in the Girls Rally and the Sunday School programmes.

Lesley did well at secondary school and was a class prefect all through her years. She then did some work in the accounts department where her dad worked, while she waited till her eighteenth year to do nursing training. That was a three-year course at Greenlane Hospital in Auckland. While there, Lesley attended the Gospel Hall at Ellerslie and entered into the life of the church, making some lifelong friendships. She did a six-month course in midwifery before another two-year Bible Training at the Bible College in Henderson. One of her favourite lecturers there was Mr Burrows who was a man who walked close to the Lord. He seemed to instil in Lesley something of the greatness, the mighty power, the holiness and loving kindness of God. They were the attributes she spoke often about to me, our children and to Bible study groups we led for some years following our marriage.

It is rather wonderful how God brings families together. I realised that with our pending marriage, He would be linking me with another family, some of whom were on this earth long before I was. Yet God would work out His plan for us as He did for all the wonderful people in the families that had gone before us. Before we were engaged, I asked the Lord if going with Lesley was the right path for me. The word from the Bible came strongly to me, The Lord says: *'Ask for the old godly way and walk in it.'* I was having my quiet time and praying to the Lord and was ready to get my concordance and see where the text was in the Bible. I knew it was in the Old Testament somewhere and it would be easy for me to look it up. I had read through the first three chapters of Jeremiah. The next day I would be reading the next three chapters. I asked for the Lord's confirmation. Sure enough, I rejoiced the next day as I read the verse that gave me the assurance in chapter six and verse sixteen of Jeremiah. I had no doubt that God who created us, brought us together to walk in His path.

CHAPTER 6

On the day of our wedding, the 12th of August 1967, there were two ceremonies. The morning was hot and fine but a typhoon was in the area. There was a number three warning which meant be prepared as there would be strong winds. Three was the first and lowest warning. In Hong Kong, the place needed to be registered and not the person performing the wedding ceremony. We went to a registry office in Kowloon and a lady magistrate performed the deed for us in about three minutes flat and we were legally married. John Short was best man, so he and Janice attended as witnesses. I was still flatting with John until we were married. He and I were dressed in grey summer suits, narrow ties and pointy shoes as was the fashion of the day.

In the afternoon we had arranged to have a church wedding at the newly opened Peace Clinic in Kwon Tong about eight miles from Kowloon. We had invited friends, both European and Chinese, and about fifty people were present. We asked Willie McVey to conduct the proceedings, which he did very well. Willie and Betty had arrived in Hong Kong from Malaysia some months before, with their two children. They were missionaries there before making their home in Hong Kong. Lesley was radiant, and it was a very special and memorable day for us. Because of the approaching typhoon, several were unable to attend, but though the wind was gusting at times, it didn't give us any problems.

We booked a hotel room for our first night at Repulse Bay and the next day took the ferry across to Cheung Chau Island where we stayed four nights in the holiday house there. Then we spent some time with Lesley's family, seeing some of the sights and shops. When they left to go home, we took a couple of weeks break up on Lantau Island. It was a place where several missionaries had purchased small stone cottages as retreats from the heat of the lower climate of Hong Kong and Kowloon. Here we were three thousand feet up, in the clouds a lot of the time, but when it cleared the views were spectacular. There was a fresh water swimming pool there, and lots of places to walk. As a bonus, there was good fellowship with the others and communal meals for lunch and dinner.

We soon settled into married life and a routine for the work we were in Hong Kong to accomplish. Lesley finished her formal language studies giving her a good grasp of basic Cantonese. She did lack some of the Biblical language for teaching the Bible in Chinese, but when she was asked to take lessons in the school where we lived, she soon picked up the necessary terms to get the messages across to the primary age children she taught. Lesley thoroughly enjoyed those teaching sessions.

My main work by day was Emmaus and Scripture Gift Mission. In the evenings and at weekends we were involved with the local youth group that was run from High Rock School. In the school catchment area were several villages, each housing up to two or three hundred people. Parents were keen to have their children educated and even if very poor would try all they could to earn enough money to pay the school fees. At that time there was a waiting list for education in almost all schools, and because High Rock was a 'Christian' run school, many of the children were sponsored from overseas, otherwise they would have missed all schooling at primary age. The youth group attracted some of the school pupils and others came from the closer villages particularly if they knew something special was on involving food.

There were picnics which consisted of walking a mile or two to a place by a stream where we could have a fire in the wet season for cooking chicken on a stick. The chicken wings, previously coated with honey, came out charcoal black. This was a first for most of these kids and they talked about it for days. A Chinese picnic was only finished when all the food was eaten and, for most groups, loud music – Chinese style – was a prerequisite to the enjoyment of the day out in the 'quiet' countryside. We never did figure that one out.

Sometimes we also organised small camps at the school for these youth. It was there I started to learn from the local people their fear of evil spirits. Some of the older boys told me later how, at night, they would wake up with a terrible fear and shaking. The ones who were Christians learned to ask for God's protection and this gave them peace, but others were not able to do this. So, if a youth was giving trouble at camp, I only had to threaten them with a night in a room by themselves and they would behave. However, in further discussions, I learned that the evil was most prevalent when the person concerned was very tired and I know I am more vulnerable to sin's temptations when I lack good sleep.

After our marriage, living at High Rock Christian School meant we were on the spot, which made it much easier for us to become more locally involved. It would have been relatively easy for us to start a church at the school but together with Francis and Ruth we made a deliberate decision not to because it would have been a 'school church' associated always with the place and the people who lived there. A local church that would last and grow needed to be operated and owned by the locals.

A few hundred yards from the school was an old walled village called Chung Tai Uk – Chung's village or house. The Chung family had built the walled village in against the hill with thick walls, a cobble stone courtyard in the middle with a well at either end and more rooms for living in and storage spaces at the back. The two feet thick stone walls were two stories high with a flat roof accessible by stairs. On the roof were places from which to fire cannons at any intruders. The building – built about 1810 – has been kept as an historic monument, but when we were there about two hundred people lived in its confines. It was about a hundred yards long and fifty yards deep with a paved area inside the walls running the length of the building. There were three main entrance doors. Rice paddies and vegetable gardens spread out in front of the building.

At the village we obtained permission from the village elders to screen gospel movies on the white wall outside. TV was only just coming into Hong Kong but was rare out in the country in those days. The films would be advertised through the school and people would bring their own seats or stand and watch. These film nights had a novelty aspect to them, but it was a good way to teach about the true God in their own language to willing viewers. We had crowds of upwards of two hundred at a time.

Michael Brown met a very keen Chinese Christian who wanted to plant a church. He had no previous experience in this and neither did Michael. Daniel Yu was self-taught in the Scriptures, with an excellent grasp of English but taught himself in the knowledge of the Bible by reading some good works in both languages, many of which cross-referenced the Bible. He was using as his example a former evangelist/preacher in China by the name of John Sung, who was considered by many to be the greatest evangelist China has ever seen. Sung died young in 1941 but not before some hundred thousand people had come to life in Christ under his ministry from about 1930. Anyway, Daniel modelled his life on John Sung and was fearless in his preaching and teaching. Daniel was a couple of years younger than me.

We got on well together even though his zeal for evangelism was far different from mine. I often went with him for open air preaching in the villages around where we lived. He used a megaphone at times, though his voice was very strong. He also had a musical bent and played a small accordion and a saw with a bow to attract attention. Daniel lived a very frugal lifestyle, was fervent for the Lord and expected the Lord to return at any time, encouraging the young people to give up their education and spend all their time in work for the Lord. I was able to bring some sense to bear on that subject and the young people soon went back to their studies. While the Lord's return is expected at any moment, He still tells us to keep occupied until He comes.

At one village a family of four teenage girls committed their lives to the Lord. Their parents owned a shark fin processing factory at their home, and their daughters worked seven days a week in the process of salting drying and shredding the fins for processing into the 'delicacy' of shark fin soup, which all good Chinese eating houses sold on their menu.

A small group of people came to the Lord at one village and were baptised. Some other young believers in the area wanted a stable church so they linked together to form a nucleus for forming a church together with contacts from the ministry of the school at High Rock. We inquired about renting a place where we could meet and found two rooms – ground floor and upstairs – in the Chung Tai Uk village. Lesley and I paid the rent and bought sixty folding chairs and a couple of other small items of furniture for the lower floor meeting area.

This was an enriching time for us as people were giving their lives to the Lord and growing in their walk with Him and encouraging their friends and family members to hear the gospel message.

A young man in his early twenties started attending in the early stages of the church. He lived locally and was the eldest in a family of seven. His father was a drug addict and John Ho financially supported his whole family. He became a strong leader in the growing church and was a stable influence on Daniel in those early days. He had a good position as an officer in the water authority.

There was opposition. These were the years of the Chinese Cultural Revolution. When we went out on the streets or in the local villages the Communist and Nationalist flags were flown in houses and shops and you knew who were loyal to either the Government of Mao in China, or Chang Chi Tsek in Taiwan. Some of the villages we went to were strongly Communist and Daniel, being who he was, had to preach there too. One evening there was a crowd of children listening to the story he was presenting when a young man came striding into the group and grabbed a small boy of about four years old, yelled at him and slapped him across the face both sides and dragged him away while the little boy bawled very loudly. The remaining boys and girls soon all left. We were sadly disappointed as we walked home. I wondered if it was like the disciples shaking the dust off their shoes when they left a village that would not accept the message of life in Jesus. I have often remembered that scene and reflected on the agony of the child and how or what ever happened to the youth in his late teens who intervened as he did. Parents of the young people often made it difficult for their offspring to attend church. That was one reason for having services on Sunday evenings, so they could attend after work.

Some young people were unable to be baptised because their parents would not allow it. Within the group there was a lot of pressure put on them to be baptised and in hindsight I think some of this should have been handled better for those who were put in that situation. As the church started to get on its feet, they wanted to become more influenced by their own Christian culture. The singing was an example of this. A lot of Hong Kong Churches at that time used hymn books which were translations of English hymnals. These young people were writing their own songs and or using direct Chinese Christian songs set to Chinese music.

Not long after the church started, they wanted to reach out to the lost around them. It was decided that they would go and preach to the crowds who went to the local Buddhist temples. It was a public holiday, and this was one of their important festival days when people offered food to the spirits of their departed ancestors. This is how I remember that day.

We met for early morning prayer. Three teams were to go to different places to witness to the crowds. It was a public holiday and a festival that took place in the cooler months. The team I joined was targeting the 'Ten Thousand Buddha' temple on the hill above Shatin village. The plan was to join the throng going up the steep winding narrow staircase to the temple's open grounds at the top. It was a crowd of bustling noisy people slowly winding their way up the path – parents, all age children from babies on backs to teenagers, struggling elderly and lots of middle age men and women, many of whom would have often made this annual pilgrimage. The temple was about two hundred yards from the railway station up a steep narrow path which was crammed with humanity all dressed in freshly washed clothes to mark the occasion. Our team joined this noisy throng and slowly followed the crowd. It took twenty minutes before we arrive at the top and could look back to the train station to see another full train disgorging another load of people who would join the end of the queue to wait their turn to go and see the gods they worshipped.

I had been once before to see this so-called 'famous' temple. The courtyard was fenced with an eight-foot high, thick concrete fence in a dirty faded yellow paint. At the gate entrance, you stepped into a large flat area and all around the fence were ugly large plaster painted animals, elephants, cows, lions, monkeys and such. There were a few flowering hibiscus shrubs among the animals. The beauty and colour of the flowers screamed out at the tardy images of faded paint beside them. All the animals were exaggerated out of reality in size, colour and shape.

The temple building was about fifty yards from the main gate entrance. Inside the main building was a very large gold painted Buddha statue in pride of place on his stage near the back. The blue white-incense smoke wafted around, the smell of which in my mind has always been associated with darkness, and the obvious idol place of worship accentuated this evil. When my eyes became accustomed to the dim light my gaze went up the high walls. I became aware that this was a high square building and all around the walls were shelves on which were neat rows of fifteen-inch-high golden Buddhas. The name gave it ten thousand and while I hadn't stopped to count them, it was an impressive sight. There were orange-robed monks with total shaven heads in attendance and some Chinese people burning their incense and offering food in front of the large Buddha whose image was an exact replica of all the others around the walls. Who needs to worship multiple images made with human hands? Our group was there to try and show them another way.

I was the only foreigner in the courtyard when we arrived. A large crowd was already at the main door waiting to enter so our team chose a spot to start preaching. I was quite uncomfortable with the intention as we were in a public/private place without per-mission. My friend – Daniel Yu – was quite adamant that wherever we were God was there and this was his ground and idol worship was totally against God's way. So, Daniel took his portable mega-phone and started shouting out about the living and true God of heaven. A crowd started to gather. They looked stunned at what was happening, and then from the main building several of the monks streamed out and confronted Daniel. There was shouting pointing and much anger and a very heated exchange before Daniel and the group retreated. I thought there was going to be a brawl. It was close. In my opinion nothing was accomplished that would draw people to know Jesus, but the group did learn some valuable lessons from the experience.

I have never seen direct confrontation working in God's favour in my time as a Christian. Some make use of it in the belief that if Jesus and Paul could use it then we should be able to. Jesus used great tact when dealing with Gentile people, even with Pilate. It was when He was talking with unbelieving people of His own earthly race that He confronted them with facts and words that were totally true but which they later used against Him. Jesus never once showed pride or impatience. The good news about Him is always best presented with grace and truth as He gave us that example. It was interesting to see how this young church grew and learned quickly as they were confronted with different pressures from time to time.

There was a family group of six, but it was the two older sons who were most keen to follow the Lord. They had four younger sisters and the fourth child in the family had Downs syndrome. She was about fifteen and while on her medication she functioned well. On one occasion at a gathering for church she had an epileptic fit. Her brothers knew how to handle it but some of the others wanted to pray over her for healing and they did. The girl was not healed, so this led to them looking at the Scriptures to see where they went wrong. In this process they discovered that God can and does heal the sick, but the example of Paul himself shows that at other times God has His purpose for some with their illness to continue for His glory.

In about 1970 Daniel Yu fell in love with a young lady who had recently come to the Lord from Communism. They had a short courtship and then were married. It was a difficult marriage for both of them mainly because they were so far apart in their spiritual journeys, and because both were intense people. The new bride suffered from depression when under stress. Daniel put it all down to God's plan for him because John Sung had experienced problems in his marriage also. The young unmarried people in the church learned some valuable lessons from the experience as they watched and many of them made strong and secure relationships with their life partners.

When Daniel and John Ho knew we would be leaving on home leave, they asked us who was paying the rent for the rooms. We told them it was us and they said it should be the church. We totally agreed and from then the church operated as we believe it should have without any direct 'foreign' financial help. We were delighted that the suggestion came from them and they took up the responsibility and ran with it as a church. The other thing that was pleasing to us is that as a church they soon became independent of 'missionary' help.

I had been five years in Hong Kong without a break to see families or home churches, so with our ten-month-old baby Rosemary, we sailed towards Australia on the P&O liner, *Canberra*. She was a modern newer ship and was much larger than the *Oronsay* we both left our home shore on. Because of her size the rough seas seemed less formidable, though it was a relatively calm journey. On this voyage we couldn't have meals together because of the need to look after Rosemary. We were probably over protective of our first child, but she was not used to strangers at that point in her young life.

Our first stop was Sydney where we were able to see and spend an afternoon with the Guyatt family who were such a help to us in Hong Kong. Ray was settled into SGM in Sydney but he still worked every spare moment and was a person who didn't know how to relax. From Sydney we sailed on to Melbourne. A good contingent of my family was there to meet us. It was good to see them after so long away, to meet some of their offspring I had not known before and to see so much growth in those I remembered as small children. They met Lesley and Rosemary for the first time also. When finally, we disembarked we went to Graeme and Eleanor's place and then to my parent's farm at Nambrok.

For the next six months we stayed on the farm and from there visited friends, families and churches who had supported us while we were in Hong Kong. We told of the ministry that was happening and encouraged people to pray for the new church and the individuals at Shatin. In this process we visited churches in Gippsland and in most areas of Victoria. My parents had purchased a Peugeot car for us to use and they lent us a small ten-foot caravan they owned, for our time around Victoria. They were extremely generous to us and we greatly appreciated all they did.

We had a meeting in Underbool, which was about three hundred miles northwest of Melbourne. At the farm where we stayed there was a plague of mice and as we drove on the road there were mice running across the road every few yards. They ate the wheat crops of the area and caused a lot of destruction. At the same farm I walked in a sheep paddock with the farmer and asked him what the sheep ate as it appeared all bare dirt to me. He scraped up a handful of burrs and seeds and told me there was plenty of food there for the sheep. He had merinos and they were the same colour as the red dirt they lay on.

Next day we had the distance to drive to Melbourne as I had a meeting to speak at that evening. We left as early as possible. There were times when we travelled at just over sixty miles an hour with the caravan on behind and a couple of times when wind gusts caught it and it swayed from side to side. The roads were all flat and straight with hardly any traffic, much different to what we were used to in Hong Kong. We were in the outer suburbs of Melbourne with only a few miles to our destination. We had been through a set of lights and were picking up speed when there was obviously something wrong with the van as there was a loud rattling noise from behind.

To my horror the tyre had blown out and the wheel had come off the stub axle. The van was on a lean, but I was able to jack it up, take out the offending wheel with its wrecked tyre. The wheel nuts were inside the hubcap, so I was able to put the spare wheel on and finish the journey. There was no damage to the van, just the tyre. How thankful we were that this had not happened away out in the country when we were travelling much faster. 'My heavenly Father watches over me,' were appropriate words of a song for us then and they still apply every day.

We arranged by letter two weeks of meetings in Tasmania, which included six or seven meetings per week. Usually there were at least two on a Sunday and sometimes three. Mondays were usually free but Tuesday, Wednesday and Thursdays there was mostly a meeting arranged and often Friday or Saturday night to a youth group. We mostly stayed with people in their homes.

We had driven the car to Melbourne and had caught the ferry to Devonport. We arranged time with Aunty Clair, ate dinner with Uncle Geoff and Aunt Betty in Ulverstone and took a meeting at their church. Smithton, Wynyard, Burnie and Sheffield were some of the places we visited. We were also asked to visit several other relatives while there. Launceston and Hobart were also included in the visit. Lesley was pregnant at the time, so we were limited in what was wise to do. It was unsettling for Rosemary with us moving about so much.

Back at Nambrok, my parents were really getting to know Lesley and Rosemary. Rosemary was over a year old but was walking and starting to talk words and short phrases. Mark used to come often and play with her. She loved the farm life. One day she was playing with the handle of the rotary clothes line though she could only just reach it. There was a spider web underneath the handle, so I thought I should remove it. There was a nest of about six red back spiders in the web, which I quickly disposed of. The redback spider is the deadliest spider in Victoria. We were glad Rosemary didn't disturb them. I wondered how long Mother was using the line with the spiders so close?

At the time Jim was managing the farm and I milked the cows for him while they took a few days off for a holiday. Pete and Joyce were in the pine forest over at Flynn a few miles away and David and Barbara were on a farm at Kurumburra, which was sixty miles from Nambrok. Graeme and Eleanor were in Frankston, and Malcolm and Nancy were in Lalor, both suburbs of Melbourne. We were able to see them all, but because of their work didn't see them often.

Home leave was not easy for us. People had expectations of us that sometimes we were not always able to fulfil. We found the travelling from place to place without any consistency to be quite difficult, probably because we both enjoy a more settled existence. It was very good meeting family and friends again, but our hearts were really in Hong Kong with the people we had been called to work among. We found the same when we were in New Zealand, except this time I was getting to know Lesley's relatives and see new places.

We flew from Melbourne to Auckland and were met at the airport by Lesley's parents. I had not met her dad before but felt I knew him after all this time. We drove down to Tauranga to stay with them before I got into deputation meetings again. Lesley's parents went to a lot of effort on our behalf. They purchased a VW

Beetle for us to get about in. In the North Island I took meetings south in Wellington and North as far as Kaikohe and Dargaville. We flew to Christchurch and stayed with Lesley's brother and sister-in-law while I took meetings in Christchurch and some other centres in the South Island.

It was encouraging to meet so many people who prayed for us and for the ministry in Hong Kong. They all were familiar with one of our colleagues – Ruth Whitehead – who was in Hong Kong since 1948, also a lady called Miss Daniel who was in her late eighties. She had been in China as a New Zealand missionary in an orphanage until the Communists took power in 1948 when she and her adopted Chinese family went to live in Hong Kong.

During the meetings in both Australia and New Zealand we had asked people to pray for one of the Chinese young people we were working among. It was amazing the number who took this up and we supplied them with a photo and a background of the person they prayed for. I believe this was probably the most significant use of our time in Hong Kong because when we returned thirteen years later, we were encouraged to hear how God was still blessing the lives of those we ministered to. This was especially true for the ones we knew were being regularly prayed for. They operated the church from a Biblical pattern as they understood it. While I did give some input after my return from a year in Australia and New Zealand this new body of believers ran the church as they deemed best.

God blessed them and multiplied them to three other churches that we knew of after our final return to Australia. One grew under Daniel's leadership to be a congregation of more than a thousand. John Ho and some others of the early group started a church in Kowloon in rooms they rented, and when he left with his wife and family to emigrate to Canada in 1995, there were one hundred and twenty people in that church that they had been instrumental in planting.

The two offices I worked from were on the second floor of an eight-storey building in Tsim Sha Tsui. It was a short distance from Kai Tak airport. We had the noise from all the aircraft, but so did thousands of other people in the area. There were shops on the ground level of the building and people living in apartments on each of the other floors. There were lifts in the building, but we only used them if we were taking delivery of parcels or such. Each office was the same layout with a small bathroom and kitchen and the other four hundred or so square feet were used for desks and storage of literature. The windows were along the outside wall only and all had steel bars across them to prevent break-ins. There was one window where we could unlock the bars and hang our laundry out the window on bamboo poles, if we had been living there.

Both these ministries operated on the principle of faith in that we didn't appeal to anyone except God for requesting finance. Sometimes though, people did ask and we would tell them of the need. Both were literature ministries. Emmaus was a Bible Correspondence School. We sent out either a booklet or loose lessons and when completed they were returned to our office for marking. Often the student would have questions that we would endeavour to answer and/or include a small booklet or leaflet from SGM to help them. Many became followers of Jesus as a result.

There were three Chinese men in the Emmaus office to do the Chinese marking when I first started there. They were kept on though there was not enough work for all three of them. I felt sorry for them as one had to go, though the situation was not easy to deal with. We prayed much about it and the Lord gave us His peace and guidance. I hope I was being a good steward of the funds that were entrusted to us for the work.

Courses were sent to most countries in South East Asia though we only printed English and Chinese. Some students were in prisons, but most were young people many of whom wanted English courses to improve their English. The exception was Mainland China because at that time there was no Christian material permitted into the country. Chinese and English readers in Hong Kong and Taiwan were the main students. We sent Chinese courses to the Philippines, Malaysia, Burma, Laos, Cambodia, and several other countries in South East Asia. The beauty of the Chinese script is that if two people could read and write Chinese, they could communicate even though they didn't understand the other's spoken dialect. There are about a hundred different dialects in Chinese with the same characters for each dialect.

In my time, one of the most memorable cases for me was a fifteen-year-old Chinese student who lived on Hong Kong Island who had taken on the English name Ellice. At first, she would finish a course a month. After several courses Ellice committed her life to the Lord with a very real sense of knowing and wanting to follow Him always. As she progressed in her knowledge of God's word, her English improved to a very good level though it was a high standard from the beginning. Her knowledge of Jesus and God's way for her was developing. One of her sisters also became a Christian and they attended church together when they were able. Her parents didn't object to their faith though they were devout Buddhists and her mother always offered food to her idol which was on a shelf in the lounge room for that purpose.

This is a normal practice in Buddhists homes, restaurants, offices and work places. When I went into such places, I could feel the power of darkness. Any young person who desired to give their life to Jesus had a constant battle with these forces of evil while they lived at home. Ellice faced this every day. Through Jesus she was victorious over the power of evil and was a testimony to all around her without any hint of pride in her life. God's grace and mercy coupled with her faith, made her a radiant follower of Christ. People loved to be in her presence.

Ellice had an operation that went wrong on her spine at about age twelve. She could only walk with great difficulty using crutches or two sticks. This affected her schooling, but she had a capable mind for reading and learning and was very quick to grasp new concepts. Her mother's unbelief and bondage in Buddhism was also a very real burden to Ellice.

In the short years she was doing Emmaus courses she told us a little of her situation by correspondence. We contacted her by phone and Lesley and I went to visit her at home and enjoyed a warm welcome. They lived in a cramped flat on Hong Kong Island, with a view over the harbour between other high-rise buildings. We were always on the lookout for people who could translate either Emmaus courses or SGM publications from English to Chinese. Ellice asked if she could help with this. At that stage she was seventeen or eighteen, and while she was eager to assist with spiritual qualifications that were right, we were not sure how she would go with this task. Her work needed to be checked by at least two others in any case. This was made clear to her. She was happy with the arrangement.

One of the young elders in the Chinese church we helped get grounded in his Christian life also desired to assist in this work. He was the eldest son of six children and his father had been into drugs for many years. John Ho was virtually the family leader who held a responsible job with the Hong Kong Government's fresh water department. Another trip was made to Ellice's home but this time it was John I took to introduce to Ellice. I'm not sure if it was love at first sight, or if they got a lot of translation work done, but I was honoured and very privileged to be able to officiate at their wedding a few weeks before we returned to settle in Australia in October 1973.

As far as the Emmaus work was concerned, I handed that to one of John Short's colleagues. He was a young man in his mid-twenties who was keen to be involved in a ministry. I am not sure what eventuated with it. However, I do know that John Ho and Ellice had a very successful marriage and when they came to New Zealand in 1996, we hosted them and their two sons in our home and it was a delight to catch up with them again. They had planted a church in Hong Kong after we left and there were about a hundred and twenty in fellowship when they left to emigrate to Canada.

SGM was quite a different ministry to Emmaus. I was managing the work in Hong Kong on behalf of the Scripture Gift Mission based in London. Most of my contact with them was by letters, and three weeks usually passed before we got an answer, unless there was something urgent. We did have visits from one of their people every three years or so and that gave a personal face to the organisation. I liked their desire to get the Scriptures into the hands of people in their own language. From Hong Kong we got to know people in Indonesia, Korea, Japan, Taiwan, Laos, Vietnam, Cambodia, Burma, Malaysia, and some of the smaller countries and islands of South East Asia. They would request Scriptures for their ministry and if they were available in the language they requested, we would post them.

Another aspect of this was organising printing quantities of publications in different languages and English and on-sending these to various countries. Getting booklets or leaflets translated into different languages and then seeing them published, was satisfying and rewarding work. I really enjoyed it. Some of the feedback was from prisoners who had been helped by the Bible portions they read, from military personnel on service in the Vietnam War, from chaplains, missionaries, churches and from people who could use many thousands if we could supply them. Finances and the cautious approach of SGM, were a restraining influence on these requests particularly if we didn't know the person or ministry concerned.

The Chinese assistant in SGM worked part time. He had come from China with the flood of refugees when Mao first came to power in the late 1940s. He was about fifty years old and a good worker. Lui Bo Hung had four small children when I first got to know him. His was a very hard life in China and he was still struggling to get ahead as were so many of the Chinese.

About a year before we left Hong Kong we started thinking and praying about what we would do next. It appeared to us that the small church that started in the late sixties was functioning well without us and this is what we wanted to happen. We looked for people to take over the two literature ministries we were caring for – SGM and Emmaus – as these, we believed, should be in the hands of the local people. We considered the option to return to Hong Kong and move to another area to help plant a church, or even or go somewhere else in Asia. However, we kept coming back to the need in Australia and that we should go there. It seemed the Lord was opening the way for us, so we started making plans to leave.

I was surprised at the openness with me, when I told the Chinese helper I worked with in Scripture Gift Mission that we were leaving Hong Kong. Normally the Chinese would mostly tell you what they wanted you to hear. He told me I was crazy to be leaving, because I could make a good life for my family in Hong Kong. All I had to do was to get a servant or two to do the work, write reports to people at home and make a good story, with pictures, about what was happening. He listed some missionaries whom he perceived were doing just that. The sad thing for me was that the Chinese people we were trying to 'live like Jesus' among quickly discerned who were God's true followers. Faithfulness to God needs to be seen in every area of my life if I am truly living like Jesus. It is amazing, that though I often fail my Lord, He never fails me or forsakes me and is always waiting for me to draw near to Him again.

The last few weeks were hectic. We gave away most of our furniture, and the flat we had was used by an American couple who came shortly after we left. We packed all the stuff, had tearful farewells especially among the young Chinese church members who were our brothers and sisters in Christ. It was hard to leave them as we had watched them grow and mature in the Lord. We would miss the next phases of their Christian lives and ministry, but for them to reach full maturity we needed to let them run their own race.

Leaving that small growing church in Hong Kong was probably the hardest part of us leaving the colony. We found lots of joy and encouragement as we watched young lives grow and develop in the Lord. We laughed and cried with them, visited them in their homes, shared meals together, sang and worshiped the Lord together and all the while we were encouraging them to be independent of us. It was a sad day when we left because we were leaving behind a young church that we loved dearly. However, the sadness was mixed with joy because we knew the Lord was with them and would show them the way forward. And He did.

The story has a good reason why. One of the very best things we did for the young church was to take photos of them as individuals and get sponsors for them in Australia and New Zealand. In Hong Kong we were very familiar with child sponsorship helping children in their education and upbringing. We asked people to commit to pray daily for the person whose photo and name we gave them. They had no financial commitment or anything but to daily pray for 'their' Daniel, John, Ellice, Grace, Wai Hing, Wai Chung or the names of the one they were committed to.

In 1986 we had a four-day visit to Hong Kong on our way to a conference for SGM in London. It was thirteen years since we left Hong Kong to return to Australia. So many changes took place in those years, but our greatest joy was to meet again those who had followed the Lord when we were there. Some moved away but were going strong in their faith. Others were ministering in churches they helped to establish away from Shatin. The ones God greatly blessed were those who enjoyed strong prayer partners in Australia and New Zealand. Prayer really matters.

CHAPTER 7

We left Hong Kong permanently on a cool October evening in 1973 aboard the *Ocean Monarch*. This was a British Shaw Saville line and we had not travelled with them before. However, this ship was going to Wellington and was the only one at that time. We wanted to be in New Zealand to have Christmas with Lesley's family before going to Australia to make our new home there.

Our first port of call was Manila. The ship tied up while we were having breakfast and we were staggered to see armed guards with guns all along the corridors and the exits. We were met by a friend who was with Gospel Literature Outreach in Manila. He showed us some of the sights and took us to his home for lunch and then back to the ship. The ship sailed in the evening and the next day we watched some of the more southern islands of the Philippines glide by in the distance. We were headed for Rabaul in Papua New Guinea (PNG).

Right on schedule we arrived in Rabaul. The early morning harbour entrance was stunning as we watched the palm trees and people on the pristine shore going lazily about their daily chores. We anchored with that view before us and a high volcanic cone to the west which was emitting steam just to show it was still ready to spew out its fury when the time was right. Not for us that day thankfully.

We decided to go ashore and just wander, but an Aussie-born local put us and a couple of other passengers into his small wagon and took us on a three-hour sightseeing tour. It was fascinating. He gave us a good overview of the Island, and the history of the occupation of Japan during the war. We saw the relics of their aircraft on a stand overlooking the harbour. Our almost pristine ship, white in its splendour, dominated the turquoise blue water, while the smoky mountain was dominant among the jungle on the other side of the harbour. The local people suffered a lot under the hands of the Japanese occupation. Relief came as the USA and Australian forces under General MacArthur, re-captured the islands which later became part of PNG.

In Sydney we spent time with the Guyatts. It was so good to catch up with them since we last met. Ray was as busy as ever filling in every spare moment he had with work or something to do. Our next and last stop on the *Ocean Monarch* was Wellington where we were met by Lesley's family. Her parents, Janice and Gary and Maurice were all there to meet us. We stayed a couple of nights with Janice and Gary at their home in Porirua. Maurice brought his vehicle to ferry us back to Tauranga and Lesley's parents had their car there too. Our plan was to stay in Tauranga until Christmas and then fly across to Victoria and make our home there for the foreseeable future. We would have a family Christmas with the Browns, as we were uncertain how long it would be before we saw them again.

Lesley's parents rented a beach house for us at Mount Maunganui. It was a very old house in Commons Avenue. After we de-fleaed it, this place suited us very well. The house was only a couple of hundred yards to the beach. As it was an old place with old furniture and nothing pristine or breakable, it suited our small children well. Rosemary at almost five years learnt to play her first little tune on an old piano. I spoke at two of Lesley's commending assemblies, telling of our second period in Hong Kong. We had a good break before we flew to Melbourne on the 27th of December 1973.

From Melbourne we travelled by road to my parent's farm at

Nambrok. Next day was Rosemary's fifth birthday. Some of her Australian cousins were meeting her for the first time and with all the changes of our recent ventures, it was all a bit much for her. We lived in the small unit at the back of the house and the children settled well to the farm life and all that was happening there. This was their first real experience on the farm for Richard and Christine with a big veggie garden, animals, dogs and baby puppies, hens, egg collection, cows and farm machinery. Rosemary commenced school at the Nambrok country state school about a mile along the straight road that ran along the west boundary of the farm.

It was a happy time for us on the farm. The children were learning lots of new things and getting to know their cousins and other set of grandparents. At the time Lesley was not very well. Before we left Hong Kong, she had a spell of illness probably brought about by stress and this was taking her some time to get to grips with. Farm life and the relaxed kind of life style suited her well. Through the harvest period on the farm, I was able to help out and earn some much-needed cash. We had rent-free accommodation and my parents provided us with the use of a small car, but we wanted to pay our own way.

Before we left Hong Kong, we were in touch with a church in Geelong where we thought we may be able to assist if we were to live there. Soon after we arrived in Victoria, we visited Graham Young who was a cousin and one of the leaders of this new church. Graham told us that while they would value our help, there was no real opening for us as all the folk were content and actively involved with the tasks before them. Our intention if there was anything we could do in the church, we would move there, rent a house and I would look for some work in the area.

As we drove back to Nambrok it became clear to us that this was a closed door, and in our disappointment, we were not sure why. It was three months later we learned that several hundred workers were laid off work in Geelong. If I had found a job, I too would probably have been laid off. Another incident where we realised God was working out His best plans for us, though at the time we didn't know why.

I wanted a permanent job so applied for the ones I thought may have suited. We applied for a state house, five of which were being built, six miles away in Rosedale. I got an interview for a salesman job at Maples in Sale and was given the position to start on the 1st of March 1974, which was a few days before Easter. Just prior to the commencement of the job, Christine, who was just over a year old, and Richard had developed high fevers with flu-like symptoms. We took both to the doctor who gave the same medication thinking their bug was the same. However, as soon as we were back home Christine went into a convulsion and when Lesley phoned the doctor, he told us to take her immediately to hospital and he would phone ahead. The hospital was about twenty miles away. When we got there Christine was put straight into emergency and we left her there while they did tests on our unconscious daughter. In the early morning of the second day, they rang to tell us she had meningitis. From when she was admitted we didn't know if we would bring her home alive, but we left that part to our heavenly Father as we prayed and wept together.

On that day's visit, Christine at last recognised us. The doctor took us aside and told us that apart from penicillin Christine would have died and even now there may be some brain damage. She was in hospital for ten days. Richard and Rosemary were both admitted too. Richard to have his infected ears washed out, and Rosemary because she had developed similar symptoms to Christine, and the doctors were taking no chances, though both were okay with only a night in hospital. Fortunately, after Christine recovered, she had no after-effects of having been so close to death. We give thanks to God and to those who administered the treatment. It was quite a shock to us when we got a huge bill from the hospital for almost one thousand dollars. At that time a new house could be bought for about fifteen thousand dollars. Because we were only been in the country for three months, we were not yet eligible for the medical insurance scheme. We couldn't pay this off without a loan. It's here where my younger brother Malcolm, went to someone he knew in the government on our behalf and got us exempt from the payment. Another miracle for us.

Christine got the measles after she came home from hospital. Rosemary and Richard followed. I was feeling unwell and went to the doctor and he laughed at me and told me I had a child's disease. I started my new job at Maples a few days before, so was embarrassed to have to ring the manager and tell him. I was given a week off work, and was glad for the break because I was quite sick.

During this time, we were wondering what it was the Lord wanted us to do in relation to working with one or two other couples to help start a new church somewhere within Australia. Before we left Hong Kong, this is what we believed we were to do when we returned. After the Geelong door closed and I had a job in Sale we prayed about maybe renting a house in the town of Maffra where there was no evangelical witness at that stage. A young Scottish immigrant couple who had become Christians were travelling from Maffra to Nambrok to the services on Sundays. We figured if there were two families living in the town of about eight-thousand people, we may become the nucleus of a ministry there. Jock was a chemist in the dairy factory. The manager wanted him to mix the tests of the butter fat so they wouldn't have to pay some farmers so much money. Jock refused and was asked to leave. He applied and won a position in Queensland with much better prospects and higher pay and within a month of us considering this possibility they moved to their second home in Australia. Amazing how God leads His people. For some He opens doors and others He closes them as they walk with Him.

Our application for the state house in Rosedale was still unanswered and we were considering the possibility of moving the church from Nambrok to the more populated Rosedale where two church couples lived. However, when we did make this suggestion to those involved in the church, they were very reluctant to move. For some unknown reason to us my parents insisted that we move from the small unit into their bigger house. We were very reluctant to shift as the small unit suited us well. We expected by this time to be well on the way to occupying one of the houses in Rosedale.

Father was quite unwell and could do very little in terms of work and Mother wanted to go on a trip to Tasmania. She was doing all the driving at this time and they decided to go for a couple of months about the beginning of December. Father told me he was only going to please Mother. I probably got closer to my Father in those few months than ever before. It was good for us both as we discussed some of the deeper things of life.

He became more ill after Christmas in Tasmania, and died just after his sixty-fourth birthday in Devonport. As many of his immediate family who could attend, went for his funeral in Devonport where he was laid to rest. Mother had five of her six sons and their wives, together with some of her grandchildren, and her own living siblings for this sad time we all went through.

On her return home she was restless and alone though she had some of us nearby. It wasn't long before she asked us to move out of her house and find our own place. We found a tiny cottage in Rosedale to rent. Rosemary started at Rosedale Primary in February 1975. As soon as we moved to Rosedale a man in the church said to us, 'Why didn't you tell us you needed a house in Rosedale? I have just sold one there for eight thousand dollars.'

We had a look at the outside of the house, and it would have suited us well, but now it was too late. Lesley contacted the Housing Corporation – state house people – about our long-standing application and was told, 'You will have to apply for a house in Sale because that is where your husband works.' It looked like all the doors we were trying to open were closing for us.

'What have you in store for us now, Lord?'

My job at Maples was going well. At first it was a culture shock for me to be working in a store with twelve other people who were such a mixed bag of characters. Half of them had booze parties from Friday night through to Sunday, and often came to work on Monday with major hangovers.

Maples built a big new shop on a more accessible street. It could hold lots more furniture, carpets and electrical goods. I had been employed at first for the purpose of the new store. It was interesting to be part of the setting up and getting ready for this, but from the manager's point of view it was a means for his climbing up the ladder and he would do anything for a sale. There was no real joy or future in this for me, but I learned a lot while I was there. Australians are a tough people. They are largely brash, proud and boastful. But as amongst every race, there are some real genuine gems of people who show respect for others whom they live among.

I was able to purchase some furniture and fridge through the firm discount I got while working there. It was a job that was starting to set me up for the yet unknown future. In the new shop I was given the job for the pricing of all the items that came into the shop. I got to know, through the invoicing, the different manufacturers around the country. Occasionally the boss would get me to put a higher mark up on some items, and when we moved to the new shop some things got much higher mark ups than we had used in the old premises.

My brother Malcolm was working in Melbourne for a firm selling Honda cars. He suggested that I buy a small Honda Civic car at wholesale price for getting us around. The firm had several on order from Japan. The day came when he delivered the car which proved to be ideal with our small family. And another provision from the Lord.

A few weeks after we moved to Rosedale Lesley's mum became quite sick. Her recovery was slow and she became worse. Because she had no family nearby, we seriously started weighing up all the options open to us. Taking all things into account, we began to think we were in the wrong place, although we were sure God wanted us in Australia for my father's death at least. We looked back at the closing doors for our ministry and living, and it all seemed to be ending up that we go to live in New Zealand. We prayed and we had peace about the decision. The Lord was truly directing our path, just like He promised. We informed our family and I gave notice at work. We packed our few possessions for shipping to New Zealand including the Honda Civic Car we had bought. We flew out of Melbourne in early July 1975. The goods we sent arrived in Tauranga. I needed to travel to Auckland to collect the car.

Lesley's parents met us in Auckland and we travelled through to Tauranga that same day. Before us was a whole new start on our unknown journey of faith. It was important for me to find work and for us to find a house to rent in the area where Rosemary would be at school. Richard would also be starting school next term. The day after our arrival I went downtown Tauranga to go to the Labour Department to inquire about jobs. 'You couldn't have come at a worse time,' were the cheerless words that greeted me as I was handed a form to fill in. 'There are no jobs available at the moment, and they are quite hard to find.'

Before going back home I decided to walk into a couple of furniture shops. The first one I wandered into, walked around, saw a couple of staff who took no notice of me and I walked out. The second one I saw a lady on staff who asked if I needed some help and I said, 'In actual fact I am looking for a job.' I told her my circumstances. She told me to go and see the manager because someone left the day before and was not yet replaced. I arranged an interview for the next day. The boss and second in charge gave me a grilling when they knew I was a Christian. They had two Christians on staff. One was highly respected but the other would often try to witness to customers during work hours. I started my new job the following Monday. *Thank you, Lord.*

We were able to rent a house at Mount Manganui and moved in after ten days living with Lesley's parents. We were only in the house about six weeks when the agent told us it had been sold. With a three-month agreement we could have stayed but we told the agent if they found us something in the same area we would move. For the next eighteen months we rented a brick house on the main road, just around the corner from the first one.

Our church was the Mt Maunganui Gospel Chapel. It was a small group, but we enjoyed and appreciated the fellowship we had at the church over the next five years. We made some lasting friendships. During the years we lived at the Mount, life moved at a steady pace. With the small children their school times kept them well occupied. My work was five days a week and late Friday nights, and Lesley set up a small business selling the *World Book Encyclopaedia* to try and earn some extra income for the family.

When we were about a year at the Mount, Maurice – Lesley's brother – told us about some balloted sections being advertised at the Mount. In fact, they were not far from where we were living. We saw a solicitor about them and he told us to put in for all twelve sections as there would probably be a hundred applicants. If our name was called, we would be allocated the low-cost land together with a new house of our choice. Furthermore, the house and the loan were on one low interest mortgage administered by the Government Housing for people who were purchasing their first home.

Lesley attended the ballot. She found there were only sixteen applicants for the twelve sections and we were delighted to be allocated one of these. We had a three-bedroom house plan drawn up, hired a builder and had friends from the church help us with painting and decorating. We became the proud owners of our first new home. The Christian builder was so honest that when he finalised the accounts, he gave us a refund of $11.50 along with a beautiful bunch of flowers. He made a professional job of the house build. We were so grateful the way the Lord worked out His perfect plan for us, as only He could.

I put up the fences, put in paths, a garden and built a garage with a block wall between us and the neighbour. But we constantly marvel at the miracle of God's provision to get us started as home owners. Maurice loaned us money for the initial deposit on the section. However, when we sold four years later to go to Auckland, we almost doubled the price of our original purchase. It meant we were able to purchase another property in Auckland of equal value, to what we sold for in Mt Manganui.

The church we attended at the Mount suited us well. It was a small friendly place which lacked a vibrant youth work but had good children's programmes. These well suited our young family. Lesley soon became involved in these programmes. Most teenagers moved away either for education or to join other youth groups in different churches. I soon was invited to join the eldership, and we made some good friendships there.

By this time, I was approaching the forties and going through a reassessment of life and what I wanted to do. I applied for other positions, but all the time I knew I needed to be back in Christian ministry of some kind. I couldn't help looking back on my life and consider how the Lord had guided my path each step of this incredible journey. Proverbs 3:5-6 was still a key promise of assurance and hope for us as we trusted the Lord together and knew he would direct our every step. At Christies Furniture Shop, where I worked, they advertised for a new manager at Te Puke where they were opening a new store.

It was about fifteen kilometres from where we lived and I had an interview with the boss who owned several country stores in the North Island. In the process of the interview, he told me they would expect me to be able to tell a 'white lie' or two if it meant clinching a sale or making a deal. I made it clear to him that I was not prepared to do that. Hence, the job went to an outside person who within a couple of years cost them a lot of money and the store was closed. This experience of the kind of staff the firm wanted to employ, made me more unsettled than ever. I knew the Lord was still in control.

Soon after, I took a job with a church friend in his small rust proofing and water pump business. We agreed that if we couldn't get enough income for both families within a year that I would get another job. We built up the business, but it was not enough to make it viable. I got a job at the Puke Pine sawmill in Te Puke. The Christian owner of this very well run mill, died about a year before I went there but his wife kept it running with the help of successful managers. The part I worked in was producing finished timbers that were mostly shipped to Australia.

I was working on saws with a young guy whose parents had divorced and he had been shuffled around in foster care since he was quite young. Hence, he missed a lot of school and just before teenage years started binge drinking alcohol. By sixteen he was a real mess but became a Christian and was being helped by folk at the local Baptist church. When I took on this foreman role our very good working relationship immediately changed. He became angry and sullen. When I asked why, he told me he hated bosses because of so many experiences in foster homes. Our relationship was restored, and I hope I helped him work through some of the issues he held against people in authority.

This was July of the year 1981. Lesley had a phone call one evening from Cecil Grant in Wellington. He was one of the leading Brethren and chairman of several of their organisations. I previously met him while on deputation before we went back to Hong Kong. He was highly respected as a man of God. He told Lesley that there was a vacancy in Auckland for the work of Scripture Gift Mission and wondered if we may be interested. I was out, so he said he would call back the following week which he did. When I told him of our interest, he arranged to meet us at Mt Manganui.

We met and were quite open with him, telling how we had miraculously obtained our low interest home. Lesley especially was reluctant to have to give this up. However, we told him we needed time to think and pray through his proposal and said we would give him an answer one way or the other by the end August. About the 20th of August I wrote him a note asking not to hold the position open for us as we had no confirmation that it was right for us to make the move. Cecil replied, 'The end of August was our idea… keep praying.' We needed to be sure God was in this move. Our children also were reluctant to move away from their friends and familiar surroundings.

Since starting my working life, I made a policy not to ask or demand more money for wages. I have followed that right throughout my life and accepted whatever amount came my way. I suppose that made it easier to trust the Lord to supply all my needs and He has certainly done this for both Lesley and me as we have been on this journey of faith together.

Lesley and I agreed in our early life together, that if we were making important decisions, both of us would have clear assurance from the Lord that this was right for us. At our church we were studying John's gospel a chapter at a time per midweek meetings. We took it in turns to go while the other stayed home with the children. We were in chapter twenty of John and as the reading of the verses took place it was as though God was speaking to me when Jesus spoke to the doubting Thomas, *'Stop doubting and believe'* (v27). It was now clear to me that we should go to Auckland. I was quick to tell Lesley when I got home, but she quietly told me that she didn't have the assurance. We both kept praying. However, I didn't tell her my assurance was firm and I believed this was the right move for us as a family.

The next Wednesday Lesley was at the church meeting and it was John chapter twenty-one. She was unsure of the move because we were leaving a small church where we had responsibilities and we would be leaving the miracle provision of our home. The words of Jesus to Peter were the deciding factor for her. *'Peter do you love me more than these. … Follow me.'* Peter asked, *'But what about him Lord?'* (v21). Jesus said, *'What is that to you? You follow me.'* With these words Lesley was assured that the Lord could look after all the details if we followed Him. On her return home she was just as excited as I had been the week before. We rejoiced together at the faithfulness of God showing us the path ahead for the next step of our journey of faith.

We confirmed with Mr Grant that we were prepared to take the next step if the SGM Council approved our appointment. Subsequently we arranged a meeting with them in Auckland. A few days later a letter from Mr Grant informed me that I was accepted for the appointment as New Zealand Secretary for SGM starting in February 1982 with an annual salary of ten thousand dollars. It was a step of faith for us in that the salary was less than I was getting. When I started it was raised beyond what I had been getting by five hundred dollars annually. Another of God's miracles.

When we went to Auckland to meet with the SGM Council we also looked at several areas to see where we thought we might live. It was necessary to take account of the schools in the areas, and the distance to Queen Street where the office was situated. We eventually settled on Pakuranga as one of our preferred places to live. Some suburbs were not as good for both schools and the general neighbourhood areas, while others were right out of our price range.

Our next move was to put our house on the market, inform those closest to us and our work and church of our proposed move. Lesley's aged parents were in Tauranga at the time and had lived in the same house for thirty-six years. They were prepared to move to Auckland to be closer to us. Lesley's brother Maurice, was also living in Auckland.

After our house in the Mount sold, we took a couple of days and went scouting the areas to see what would be best for us. After several house inspections our last agent to call on for the day was in Pakuranga. We told the agent the price we could pay, and he took us to the only two places on his list. We looked at both. One was $6000 more money than we had though much bigger. It needed a lot of work to get it into shape. We were not sure about some of the alterations that were added. The other house was three bedrooms on the same street about fifty yards across a reserve between them. We went back to where we were staying, ate a meal, did lots of talking and praying before we had peace about it. We were on the agent's doorstep first thing the next morning to take another look at both properties. It took us only a short while to make up our minds and so we signed up for the cheaper of the two that had do-able alterations for us to accomplish. It seemed so right for us. Because this house was empty, we could move in when all the official papers went through. We settled for just before Christmas as the changeover date.

Looking back, we were amazed at how all the financials worked out. We sold the house at Mt Manganui for almost twice the original cost. We paid the loan back to the bank and opened another account in Auckland. By keeping the same amount of mortgage, there was enough money in hand to buy the property in Pakuranga. This came with a large section, beside a reserve with high poplar trees on the back boundary. It was close to good schools for the family, and within a reasonable commute for my work. We were provided with a huge personal gift by a Christchurch Trust. This enabled all the things to fit into place and we believe it was God's further miracle provision for us. We were quite amazed and so thankful. That same Trust continued to generously support the work of SGM over a number of years until the Trust founder died and it changed hands.

At home we started the packing process again. I gave notice at the mill job where I was employed, and we received an unexpected farewell gift from the church. The children were reluctant to leave their school and friends, but as parents we were confident that this was the right move for our family, and over the years ahead it proved to be so.

Some friends in Auckland kindly offered us the use of their house for two weeks while we sorted out the kitchen in the house we were moving to. This was about ten miles away but proved to be a real blessing. It also gave us time to show the children their schools and the local shopping centre. Over the next few days, we bought building supplies to fill in a large part of the kitchen wall to give better space in the kitchen. We put in a pantry and another bench, decorated all the bare cupboards and walls. The place was ready to move into about a week after the new year of 1982.

Rosemary started her first year at Edgewater College, Richard started his first year at Pakuranga Intermediate, and Christine was enrolled in the primary school just across the reserve from our house. They settled in quite quickly to their new environment. All the schools were in walking distance for them. After we moved into the house at Pakuranga, we redecorated inside room by room. I also added a new wall in the bathroom, moved the bath and that made a separate toilet room. This made the house much more liveable for us.

As a family it was a totally new life for us coming to Auckland. We were six and a half years at Mt Manganui which was like a country town compared to the hustle and bustle of the big city. Pakuranga Christian Fellowship became our church home.

At the end of 1983 and beginning of 1984, during the December-January holidays, we towed a campervan around the South Island. It was a trip we all still sometimes talk about, the rain, the glacier walks, the awesome views surrounding Mt Cook and the majestic trip across Lake Manapouri. Into early adulthood, each of our children have been back for holidays with their friends and later their own families. It is a special place.

All our three children did well at school. Rosemary's great love was for books and reading, so the library became a favourite place for her. For a birthday present in her early teens, she requested the complete works of Shakespeare and together with her Latin language learning she became quite good at English. Latin was her favourite school subject. She got part time work first with a paper round, but then in the local library. While at teacher training this also became her holiday job. Rosemary did a degree while doing her teacher training. She found exams to be easy. Music was another favourite pastime so from quite young she studied piano, and at high school had the opportunity of trying a range of other musical instruments. In her first year teaching she was the conductor of a forty-strong band of ten- to twelve-year-olds. It was a hit at their school concert. To show how good they were, the teachers from the Teacher Training Institute, brought their recruits to let them see what could be accomplished.

Richard was very competitive and worked hard all through school and on to university where he completed a four-year Civil Engineering degree. During his high school years, he took a couple of part time jobs but the one that stuck was in a civil engineering firm.

He started as the cleaner. This led to on-the-spot training while on holidays from university. On his graduation, he entered a full-time job with them. The firm were within walking distance from our home. Though his board was a token while doing his degree, he insisted on paying all his own fees for his course. Richard loved soccer and cricket and enjoyed these while he was at school. Later for holiday breaks he and several friends, and sometimes South Island relatives, would organise tramping trips. All of our three offspring were involved through their educational years with an active church youth group and some lifelong friendships were formed through this.

Christine had a different approach to educational life than her older siblings. She loved the art and craft side of school life. At a young age she could lay her doll or a teddy bear on some material on the floor and make perfectly fitting clothes for them. Later she crafted her own teddy bears. One white polar bear she has to this day. It sits in her own daughter's bedroom. At the end of seventh form, she went out to work. One of her teachers wanted her to run a costume hire business for her, but Christine found a position in a picture framing business. While there she married Wayne. After three years she went into insurance, but then decided to do a degree in design. Those years were quite a struggle for them, but she passed with honours anyway. Wayne wanted to build a house while still working as a draftsman. It was on a half-site in Howick. They lived in our caravan while this happened. It was a lovely unique house in amongst mature trees with a small stream through the property.

For the first three years of our church life in Auckland we attended the Pakuranga Christian Fellowship which was a much larger church than we were used to. We enjoyed the time there and entered into church life as much as we were able. However, there was a power struggle going on among the leadership and they were trying to discover if they wanted to be a full-on Charismatic type church or one that was more like the Open Brethren. Our children made good friends and were involved in the youth group and children's outreach on Sunday mornings. We joined a home group. I was away on SGM work for about ten Sundays of the year. Apart from that we were never really part of the church or were given any role. So, after three years we went to Howick Community Church.

This church went through a struggle time a couple of years before we arrived and they hadn't fully recovered. However, we did discover that the people who were committed to the Lord, really wanted to move forward as He directed them. This church seemed right for us. Soon we were given leadership roles. We were delighted to be part of a church that started to catch the vision of becoming a true community church. When we first attended there was a congregation of sixty people with no paid staff. When we left in 2006, they were meeting in a new church property with seating for over three hundred people. It was a vibrant, active, growing church. We had been privileged to be part the growth for more than twenty years. It became a suitable church home for our children too until they left our care in their early twenties.

CHAPTER 8

There were three people in the work of Scripture Gift Mission in New Zealand before me. Jack Burrows commenced in Christchurch in 1936 and retired in 1962. Soon after Jack Hume took over and moved the office to Auckland. He retired in 1972 and Matt Finlay looked after the office until the end of 1981 when I was appointed as the General Secretary.

Jack Burrows was loved by all and set a very high standard for the work of SGM. He worked from his home in Christchurch with wife Marjorie and kept stocks of Scriptures to send all over New Zealand, until they retired. All their records and correspondence were by hand. Telephones were not used very much either. They travelled all over New Zealand ministering to people and telling of the work of SGM. Together they laid a wonderful foundation for the work of the Mission in New Zealand. They had no children of their own. Jack died in April 1987. He was a very godly man, a powerful preacher and Bible teacher who was born in England in 1890. It was a privilege to have known them.

Marjorie died a few years after Jack and about a month before her death I was on deputation in Christchurch. I paid her a visit. She served me a cup of tea and scones in the same room as I was hosted on previous visits with the same set of cups. Then she got her old photos of SGM, and told me the story of how Jack first met her when she was twelve years old. Little did she know that after Jack's first wife died, he would go back to England and look her up, marry her and bring her to New Zealand as his wife. But he did, and they enjoyed many happy years together. To my surprise, she shared lots of other stories with me about their life together and the work of SGM. When I got a call from one of the elders in her church to invite me to participate at her funeral, I knew why I had the meeting with her just those few weeks before. Marjorie's church family were glad to be filled in with background they didn't know about. A few months later, SGM received a legacy to the value of over half a million dollars from their estate. They lived a simple lifestyle in a modest home, with only the necessities of life for their own use. However, there was laid up for them a very rich treasure in heaven for these two people who gave their lives and gifts in service for the Lord.

Jack Hume in the 1960s introduced a typewriter and made carbon copies of all his correspondence. He had an efficient lady doing the office management and keeping records. Matt Finlay followed the same system and that is what I took over. But all three of these men were good Bible teachers, and that was a skill or gift I lacked. However, just as God had helped all three of them in the various roles they filled, I was confident that He would help me too.

My work took me into the city each day to the top of Queen Street where SGM rented two rooms above a Christian bookshop at 427 Queen Street. I was working alongside Matt Finlay who retired from the work and he was to take the next six months and train me into it. Although seven years passed since I worked in SGM in Hong Kong, the system and the literature were the same with some different languages, so I was quite familiar with most things. Soon we were tripping over each other and Matt had nothing to do. His part time job assisting in another office in the building kept him occupied. The Board were happy for him to leave. London thought it was not a good idea, but it meant that I was able to get sorting out a very worn looking office with new paint and some new furniture and a good upgrade. Lesley helped for two or three days a week and was home again in time for the family to return after school.

During March I started my first deputation visits at Eastern Beach Missionary Camp. From those contacts I had invitations to visit assemblies further down country. In April we displayed SGM at Totara Springs Easter Camp. In June I went to Gisborne and Hawkes Bay with meetings at Opotiki, Gisborne, Wairoa, Napier, Hastings and Havelock North. In the daytime I visited ministers, pastors, hospital chaplains and individual people on our mailing list, besides anyone else we could contact. We did make some progress and I was meeting a lot of people who had a love for the work of SGM. This became my pattern over the next twenty or so years both in New Zealand and Australia during the times we did deputation. Lesley was able to go with me most of the time from 1988 because our youngest daughter was in her late teen years. Sometimes we would take our caravan for accommodation around New Zealand.

The Lord guided us into the work of Scripture Gift Mission for some of the most productive years of our lives, seven of them in Hong Kong and twenty-three years in New Zealand. For all this time He provided bountifully for us in every way. I never ceased to be amazed at the constant loving care and provision for the needs of the work, together with our own personal needs. We learnt so much from the Lord as He helped us lean more and more on Him instead of trying to work things out our way.

One time we needed to pay a printer's bill of one thousand dollars for some Scriptures I had printed in the Samoan language. I went home and told Lesley that we needed to tell the Lord about it. We prayed. The next day an elderly lady rode her bike to the office. When she was leaving, she hastily dropped an envelope on the desk and said it was a small gift for the work. I went to the door with her, said my farewell while thanking her again for the gift. Then I went back to what I had been doing before she came, thinking that the gift would be a small amount similar to what she had given twice before. Besides, I had been to visit her at home in a small cottage with few comforts and the rusty old bike tucked in under the eave. Mrs Smith told me about her past life with an alcoholic husband, who before his death made life very difficult for them. She was a frugal lady on a benefit. Her clothes, though clean and neat were well past the fashion of the day. I opened the envelope and saw a bank cheque for a thousand dollars pinned to a note on which words were written with a trembling hand. I was overcome with emotion and was wiping the tears away as I thanked the Lord while trying to read the note again: 'Please use this gift for printing Scriptures in overseas languages.'

People from time to time would come into the office and get their Bible portions direct, either from the stocks we held in other languages or the main supply we carried in English. One day a young man of about twenty-five came into the office looking for a suitable publication he could use for street witnessing. When I had chatted to him and he examined the suitable literature, he went out with a bundle of leaflets to try them out. A couple of days later he was back and he took away a hundred copies of *Four Steps to Life*, which was the ideal gospel leaflet for the work he was doing. He told me the Lord impressed on him the need to come to Auckland to do street work for a period. He was staying with a relative who was in a local church, which he also attended while in Auckland. I got to know him and respect him as a humble servant of the Lord who came to visit the office several times for further supplies of *Four Steps to Life,* and for prayer together. He visited me before he left Auckland and told me that three people became Christians and were attending the local churches where they lived.

When I started in the New Zealand office in 1982, and I was about to turn forty-one, we were using a portable typewriter and carbon copies. Mail delivery was also much more reliable as it was the only method, apart from expensive phone calls, for keeping in touch with people. For copying letters or other documents of quantity, they were copied on a Gestetner copy machine which was unreliable. Within four years I graduated to a desk top computer with thirty megabytes of RAM and a dot matrix printer. Later I had my first Laser printer. We were using dial up for telephones, and fax machines were not known then. When fax came in, we could communicate with overseas offices much quicker. But it was e-mail that made communication and sending documents so much easier.

The office in New Zealand was responsible for distribution in Fiji, Samoa and Tonga, where most of our overseas contacts were. These three island groups were the easiest to get to by air. Sometimes we would get requests from the other islands. One I remember was from Kiribati where a Gospel boat had been visiting and distributing some of our publications. A teenage boy wrote and said in his letter how he came to trust the Lord through reading the *Way of Salvation* booklet, he was given by people from that boat. A Christian man from Tuvalu requested publications for people in his homeland which he visited often, although he worked in Fiji. The Fiji Gospel School used many booklets and leaflets for their students right though out the classes. The Director of Scripture Union ordered quite a large shipment of a series of six illustrated leaflets dealing with issues of youth, drugs, violence, the occult, etc. He gave each student their own copy after each period of Bible teaching in high schools around Fiji.

There was a Fijian lady who had a very effective work in the women's prison. She was anxious to get more Scriptures to the Fijian and Hindi women whom she worked among. We formed excellent working relationships with the Bible Society, Scripture

Union and some other mission groups. In Samoa there was a vital ministry by Youth for Christ among the young people. I enjoyed most, the hospitality in the homes of Christians. Some were very poor and lived in corrugated iron shelters with no internal lining and little food. They each had something else which was, their deep love and trust in God. For me, to meet with other believers from different churches and backgrounds was a foretaste of what heaven will be like.

The three publications that gave me great satisfaction in publishing were *Daily Strength* in Maori, Samoan and Fijian. These were Bible readings with selected verses for each day of the month. There was always a steady call for these booklets. We usually printed five thousand copies at a time. God had His gracious, humble servants who assisted in the translation and the proofreading of these popular booklets.

My time spent with SGM, gave me a great insight into some lives of Christians in other countries. I was privileged to meet with many people of different cultures in various places I visited. Fiji, Tongan, Samoan and Cook Islanders had Bibles printed in their own languages, when missionaries came to these islands in the latter part of the eighteenth century. Most translators started with short passages of the Bible and printed the New Testament first. It would take several more years to get the remainder of the Bible finished. It is a joyful occasion in any language when a Bible or a New Testament comes from the printer, and the people have God's message for them to be able to read in their own language.

When Mr Cecil Grant died, the SGM Council lost a man who had previous experience with SGM in London. While he worked in London for the New Zealand Government for four years, he gave some of his time to acquaint himself with the work of SGM. His first-hand knowledge of the work was invaluable to both me and the other people on the New Zealand Council. This godly man led the New Zealand Council over thirty years. It was difficult to find suitable replacements and eventually London suggested that the Australian Council also be responsible for New Zealand.

For the last ten years before my retirement, I came under the Council in Sydney even though I was still responsible for the work in New Zealand. It was a very interesting time. Council meetings in Sydney were three times a year. I was asked to go to Papua New Guinea. There were also areas of Australia that had not seen a representative of SGM for some years. North Queensland was one area that needed a visit. We worked out that we could take five weeks away from the New Zealand office because we employed a very efficient co-worker who was able to handle the day-to-day work in my absence.

I took Lesley with me this time, to help with prearranged meetings in Queensland. We drove a loaned car from Sydney to Cairns and back to Townsville where Lesley stayed for ten days with my brother and his wife, while I went on alone to visit PNG.

I went to Lae to spend some time with a group of missionaries from Germany. The founders set up things so that families or individuals from their home churches could come for a short- term mission experience, or stay and be part of the enterprise. They had worked quite diligently to establish their operation. Crops and gardens supplied the local town with fresh vegetables and fruit. There was a dairy farm for fresh milk, butter, cheese and cream. These, and other revenue raising works, went towards support for forty local people they had trained to be pastors in their own villages. I had the privilege of being able to tell these pastors about the work of SGM, and hear stories they told me of how they used some of our publications to help others in their journeys of faith. A thriving book store had educational books as well Bibles in Pidgin and some other local languages that were spoken in the district. I was amazed by the range of English Bible study books available for Christians to help them grow in their walk with God.

When I met with Wycliffe Bible Translators, they were keen for us to have a joint workshop with teams of three or four selected people from small tribes who had no publications in their language. It took two years planning. This was an opportunity for them to translate a publication of stories from Mark's gospel and SGM would publish the booklets for them. Wycliffe Bible Translators had the facilities and the trained personnel to tackle this type of work. We were in one of their retreat centres in the highlands of Madang. The mornings were devoted to lectures, translated into Pidgin. Some of the students were more advanced than others. However, it was a very worthwhile project. Most of the ten groups who were there eventually had their own tribal language printed. This was a stepping stone for them to produce the New Testament in their mother tongue.

I was privileged to go to India in February 1996 for a conference with a number of SGM representatives from countries around the world. Fifteen of us were there for a time of fellowship, learning, and in particular to glean what we could about India, its culture, people and their way of life. Of course, to gain a knowledge of any country, you need to live among the people and learn the language. India as a nation is one of the most diverse places on the globe. I saw some of this when we visited a tribe of people who had a totally different language and life style to the common populace. Later, we toured a centuries-old palace to see in some of the beautiful staterooms an array of ancient furniture and tapestries. This palace was inside the confines of thirty acres. Some of the ground had lovely gardens with the bulk of them being covered with a variety of stately old trees. A seven-foot-high stone fence surrounded the perimeter, and a high gate was shut behind us as we exited from the grand palace of the Rajah's wealthy family. It seemed like we were exiting from a lost world.

Outside, life existed with all its poverty, hunger, heartaches and sorrow. If only I knew what life was like living day after day in dust, filth and unbearable heat. Without running water, no power for cooking, not knowing if there was enough food for one meal a day, and never having the pleasure of going to bed without worrying about what tomorrow would bring. Always tired, always fearful of abuse of one kind or another, always untold misery for children and adults. I saw it in the eyes and faces of little children as they clung to their mother, whose face held the same expression. Before I was ushered away, I saw some teenage boys dressed in ragged shorts only, looking our way. The same faraway look of poverty, despair and hopelessness haunted them too. Sadly, I saw much of this on my short visit. I felt powerless to do anything to help.

One incident has always stuck in my mind. I was walking along one of the main thoroughfares of Bangalore with a British colleague. The street was dusty and crowded. Beggars were sitting or loitering beside their few possessions. A young mother was squatting beside a pile of scrap paper while a baby suckled under her thin, soiled sari. A boy, about four years old, dressed only in shabby shorts was holding the hand of a younger sister as he talked with her. We walked a little distance past them to a road crossing and waited for the green light. The traffic was chaotic. Rickshaws, bikes, scooters, cars, taxis, trucks and buses, over-loaded with all sorts of goods, or too many people hanging on for dear life. Horns honked, music blared above the noisy traffic in this cacophony of sound. Amid the dust, haze and colourful beauty of the scene, a little girl came to David, my colleague, and wrapped her arm around his leg below knee level. She couldn't reach much higher, but her eyes did as she focused them on David who looked down at her. I watched as their eyes locked on each other for what seemed longer than it was. What thoughts went through their heads? David had two school-age daughters at home in London. Would this child grow up living on the streets all her life? David had moist eyes as he gently unravelled the child from his leg and we crossed the road without her. This experience still brings tears to my eyes.

It's true, there were many joyful experiences too. The conference lasted five days and was at a retreat, run by a delightful Indian couple who really looked after us. It was situated right beside a tea plantation in the southern highlands of India. We went for walks to a higher spot on the plantation for a view over the surrounding country. All below us was a haze of smog. The temperature at night was cool owing to the height of the situation. In the day time it was much hotter than we were used to, especially when we went down to lower areas. We had been told to keep the doors shut at night because tigers prowled about. One did too, but only on one of the nights we were there.

Later I went with Lesley for deputation in Tasmania for almost three weeks. We fitted in a Council meeting in Sydney at the same time too. In October of 1997 we went for deputation to Western Australia, mostly around Perth for visits to churches. From there Lesley flew back to Auckland while I went to Zimbabwe for another SGM leadership meeting. Two African nationals were by this time on the team, based in Zimbabwe and Zambia. They were both very enthusiastic to see the work grow in their native lands.

Aids was sweeping through Africa at that time. We were taken to a centre that had brought in orphans. There, a lady told us the sad story about her life with Aids. Her husband was a long-distance truck driver who came home to their wretched living conditions and infected Mary with the disease. There was no cure for it then. He died before Mary knew she was infected. You could have heard a pin drop, as Mary told us the doctor reported that she would die within a few months. The family consisted of five young children living in poverty, without enough food and no prospect of education. Mary struggled with the worry of her death and what would happen to her children after she died. Who was going to help her? Would her children be left alone, the older son of eight years old having to care for his younger siblings? Stories were being spread that this was now common practice in Zimbabwe and other African countries. Mary had tears in her eyes as her story unfolded of how she and her family were found and taken in by the overcrowded orphanage. She was given light work to do and so grateful for all that was done for her and her children.

The year was now 1998. We had been living in our thirteen-year family home at Pakuranga while our children found their own places to live. When they were well settled, we considered the possibility of an upgrade. After all the scenarios were worked through, the cheapest plan was for us to buy a section on which two separate houses could be built. We sold our family home, stored most of our furniture and were living with our daughter Christine and her husband Wayne, who helped us with negotiations. While we were on deputation in the South Island, Wayne phoned to tell us there was one double section available in the new area we were looking at. However, we needed to let the agent know the next day. It was good to ask the Lord on this matter and have His assurance. We trusted the Lord who gave us His peace. Though we were unable to physically see the site, we asked Wayne to put our name on it for us.

A few days later we saw the site and it was perfect for our needs, with a pleasant outlook away from the main roads. We got the house built on the lower section and put it on the market. However, there was a downturn in house prices at that time and it was difficult to sell. The house we planned to live in couldn't be built until we received the money from the other building. In many ways it was a stressful time until we decided to move into the house that was already built, and sell off the favoured section. Both of us believed this was the will of God. Peace settled in our hearts and we started to make plans to move. The agent for the sale of the house had a week remaining before his three-month contract expired. He was able to get a buyer for the house within that week, so we proceeded with the building of the second home, which was finished ready for us to move into about four months later.

The way Wayne designed the house for us seemed to suit our needs just exactly as were required. We were both delighted and thankful for another of God's provision. Little did we know that we would be able to have the SGM office downstairs, the young grandchildren, church small group meetings, and overseas visitors to stay. But God had something else to teach us.

Our understanding when we first entered this part of our journey was the cost for our mortgage would be more than we had ever paid before. We didn't make any profit or loss on the house we recently sold. Lesley looked after our finances, always keeping them in check. After looking at our mortgage on the monthly bank statements, she asked me if I had any suggestions to pay it off quicker. We agreed to make this a matter of prayer. I was diligent in prayer for a few days before something else came along. Unbeknownst to me, Lesley continued asking the Lord for assurance on the matter of our mortgage, because six months later she reminded me of this answer to her prayer and anxiety. Her reading that day was Jeremiah chapter 29. She said the Lord gave her the answer in verse eleven, which says, '

'For I know the plans I have for you,' says the Lord. 'They are plans for good and not for disaster, to give you a future and a hope.'

Six more months went by. Lesley trusted God, knowing that He wouldn't fail to keep His promise. She didn't know how or when, but she was at peace about our mortgage. An unexpected letter came from the Public Trust telling how a recluse uncle named Owen had left his legacy – equally – to the children of his siblings. Since serving in the Pacific Islands during the second world war, he had lived apart from his family. Lesley told me she had seen him on only one occasion – in 1958, when she was at her grandmother's funeral. Uncle Owen had been there too, but they didn't speak to each other. The legacy he left Lesley was enough to pay all our mortgage. God knows the plan he has for us, to give us a future and a hope. I wonder if God's plan worked out for Uncle Owen as it was intertwined with His plan for us? I am awestruck at the marvellous way God arranges our individual lives for His purposes.

Sometime before the new century was ushered in, the SGM leadership decided that we would divide the world into five sections. We came under the Asian and Pacific region with our capital base in Singapore. We were to centralise our annual Council meetings and all the publications we needed were to be sourced from there to save postage. Because of my previous contact with Indonesia from Hong Kong, I was invited to go with a small team and see if there was a greater need for the Scriptures. One of our main aims was to establish a better working relationship with the contacts we had. For me personally it was an eye opener to see the great need for the Scriptures in different languages, to enhance and mutually encourage many workers who were serving the Lord so faithfully through much opposition. The Australian office was responsible for Indonesia and with the help of the local people were able to develop some very successful Scriptures with illustrations for rural communities.

In December 2004, eighteen months before I reached retirement age, I retired from Scripture Gift Mission. The London management had told me five years earlier that they wouldn't be replacing me when I reached sixty-five. Everything had changed in the way we did things. Different personalities brought new ideas, with technology making life interesting and more complex. Mobile telephones were being used by business people especially. This was a sad time for us because I thought the decision to cease the work in New Zealand was not in SGM's best interest. However, several of the centres around the world closed at that time because they out-stretched what they had supported in the past. The Australian office became responsible for the work in New Zealand.

With the Lord's help I decided to do something entirely different for the next eighteen months and beyond, by starting a handyman business. I had kept up some skills as a hobby, especially with a love for working with wood. I purchased a second hand Toyota Hiace van and fitted it out with the tools I needed. Things started to fit into place for us. I soon had almost as much work as I was able to cope with. There was a variety of jobs which added to the interest. Wooden decks were needing repairs, sometimes a bathroom job was necessary and once I spent several days laying bricks and making new wooden fences and steps to a back yard. Gardening jobs were quite common. There was also a couple of jobs to do on a house that needed a bathroom alteration, the kitchen refurbished, and a low window changed to another wall in a bedroom. Considerable tiling jobs were undertaken also. I thoroughly enjoyed the times I was able to do these jobs, but I found it difficult to quote on my labour or an hourly rate.

CHAPTER 9

In October of 2005 we visited Aunty Loie at her retirement village in Tauranga. We wondered if a move to another area seemed right for us. Was it to be in Tauranga near Aunty Loie? Or should we go somewhere closer to our immediate family? We seriously looked at housing in and around the outer areas of Tauranga. It was one of our favourite places to live. At that time our three children were each settled between Orewa and Wellington. We didn't like the idea of living in Wellington. Rosemary and Keith and their three children were there, but we decided to go north somewhere near Orewa. Our house was soon ready to go on the market and Richard and Tania had recently moved to Orewa. Christine and Wayne were in Howick, not very far from where we were living.

The house we lived in for eight years sold quickly and we knew how much money we could put into another property. We were house-sitting for Richard and Tania while they were on holiday. This enabled us to search the property market. Our search took us to places fifteen miles from Orewa and to several agents in the area.

House hunting can be very disappointing. Most seemed to be out of our range or didn't have space for a caravan or room for a vegetable garden. There were none suitable in the country areas that appealed to us. After five days Lesley was discouraged and wanted a break. I was willing to go alone and continue searching. We had discussed that if possible, we would like somewhere with a view of the sea, peaceful and quiet, room for the van and a bigger garden. I thought I needed something to do in my retirement years. While driving along I prayed again, 'Lord show us the way in this and help us to find the right place to live.'

I drove out to Whangaparaoa and went to the Barfoot office again. The salesman told me some sections had just come back on the market at Army Bay. These sections were reduced by about $100,000. He gave me a map and directions. I went and had a good look. Several of the sites were perfect for our needs. We could get a site and a house built for the money we got selling the house at Howick. I hurried back and took Lesley out, trying not to sound too excited. However, she fell in love with the place knowing that we would have a sea view and all the things that were important to us.

We valued the help of Wayne and Christine who came the next day with the agent. There were many questions, but we were sure it was the right decision for us. So, we signed and paid a deposit on the site we considered best for us. Wayne was blessed with the gift of being able to look at a spare piece of land and imagine the house that would best fit the space. Together with Christine, who worked at Mitchell Homes, they developed a house plan for us and arranged all the contractors. There were only a few minor alterations we made to the plans. By February of 2006 the plans went to the local council for approval.

Toby was born to Tania and Richard on the 25th of February 2006. Lesley and I were living in our caravan at Orewa Beach Holiday Park. It was five minutes' drive to their house where I was doing some handyman work on one of the bedrooms, preparing it for the arrival of their third son. Lesley was able to give lots of help too.

When we first moved to Orewa we were praying about which church to put our efforts into. A friend at Howick asked us why we were leaving a church where we were respected and made good friends to go somewhere to start again. We didn't even think of that aspect, but after more than twenty years in the same church, we felt the Lord was calling us in a new direction. The first Sunday we attended the church where Richard and Tania went, but we knew we couldn't settle there. The second Sunday we went to another large church and although we knew people in both these congregations, we didn't feel at home in either church. So, on the third Sunday, we found ourselves in the smallest of the three churches we visited thus far. This proved to be a friendly group of people whom we were very happy to worship with. We acknowledge again that the Lord was guiding our path. After our third Sunday the pastor paid us a visit at the caravan park. We made sure to be part of a home group that met weekly. Though the church had been through some difficult times, they were starting to regroup with different people moving into the district. It became a place where we felt as if we belonged and the Lord made it clear to us that this was to be our spiritual home for the foreseeable future. It was called Orewa Community Church.

Our house was still some weeks off being started and we were booked to go to Australia for a Knowles family reunion. This took place at Rokeby where, as a young boy, I went to church and Sunday school with our family. We enjoyed the time spent with some of the family who were there. After the reunion we went to Tasmania for a ten-day holiday in a motor home.

Our son-in-law, Wayne Mitchell, was a Trustee for Adventure Specialities Trust, an agency who specialise in taking at-risk youth on outdoor adventures. They did such things as mountain climbing, white water rafting and skiing. Wayne had the task of being project manager for a property development in Whananaki, which was a three-hour drive north of Auckland. In his role as architect, he was responsible for the drawing of the site plans for the four-hundred-acre property that was gifted to the Trust by the American owner Geordie and his wife Linda. Once a year they spent several weeks with family and friends, fishing and swimming, away from the hustle and bustle in their city life in Seattle, USA.

The bay was known as Rockells Bay, named after a previous owner who had built a delightful little cottage tucked in beside a hill with large trees growing on a hill at the back of the cottage. The sea was fifty yards away from the front deck.

A few months after my retirement, Wayne asked me if we would be interested in planting trees at Whananaki. We had been there before with Wayne and we knew something of the seeming isolation. It was twenty miles off the main highway and at the end of five miles of rough, winding, gravel, though very scenic, coastal road. Lesley and I prayed together and discussed the whole proposal. We would be able to stay in Geordie's cottage, rent free, and we would have an initial three-thousand native trees to plant on the hillsides. The first sites to be developed were on about twenty acres of hilly seafront farm land. The stream that meandered its way through the lowest part of the valley and past the cottage, was fed by a spring in the bush further up on the farm.

The planting season was May to September of each year. We were totally inexperienced in tree planting, except for a few plants and shrubs we purchased for our garden. But we accepted Wayne's offer, understanding that we wouldn't need to start planting till May of 2006. The time fitted so well for the Knowles family reunion in Victoria and the holiday in Tasmania.

We were home again in the mid-April of 2006 preparing for a time at Rockell's Bay planting trees. Our plan was to live in the bach on the property and stay at least until September for the first season. Our new house was also ready to be built, but it couldn't be started before June. The plans were all drawn up and we had chosen the colour schemes, floor coverings, electrical fixtures and all the other things needed so that our house could be finished on schedule, in November.

Knowing that over the next few months, we would often be making the trip from Orewa to Whananaki, we timed the first trip to be sure the breaks met our needs for the three-hour journeys each way. Sometimes we needed to shop in Whangarei for groceries or other supplies.

The date was the 7th of May 2006 when the first truck arrived loaded with two thousand potted trees in trays of fifteen, easy to handle and ready for planting. The trees we were planting on steep hills were all natives to New Zealand and this batch were called manuka and kanuka – the names for two types of tea-tree. Later, the planting was to be on flatter ground where the creek wound its way seawards. There were forty white Charolais cattle in the flat area eating the lush grass, while they were kept in place by a one wire temporary electric fence.

We had arrived at the cottage two days before the trees were delivered. There was time to work out our strategy for the planting. Where would we start? How would we easily measure the distance between each tree and the row of trees? What about getting over the fence and carrying the trees and things needed for planting about a hundred metres down a steep, rough bank? Before starting on the venture, we put it all before the Lord and asked Him for help, guidance and protection. It is a great privilege to take things to the Lord in prayer or just talk with Him about our situation. He showed us how to make a measuring stick out of dry flax stalks that we used right throughout our time. Two short ladders in the storage shed were utilised for getting over the fences and I devised two boards with rope handles for carrying the trays of trees ready for planting. But best of all, was the Lord's protection for both us both all the time of our sojourn. Sure, blisters and aching muscles at times were endured, but there were no major falls or any incidents to cause concern. We give all the glory to our all-loving, caring God. The protection of the Lord brings to mind the words of Moses in Psalm 91:9-12,

> *If you make the Lord your refuge, if you make the Highest your shelter, no evil will conquer you; no plague will come near your home. For He will order his angels to protect you wherever you go. They will hold you up with their hands so you won't even hurt your foot on a stone.* (NLT)

At the beginning of August there was one weekend when we went back to Orewa to look for a suitable flat to rent for about three months, while our home was being built. We went to have another look at Havilah View where our house was being built. When we arrived, there were a couple with two young children looking over the low fence at the incomplete framework of our house. Lesley got talking to them. She told how we were looking for a place to rent for about twelve weeks, until the end of November when we expected our home to be completed. By this time, I was on the scene and introduced to the family. After a few minutes talking, they offered their holiday house to us at a reasonable rental if it was suitable. They invited us to walk the three hundred yards to their house with them as they were going home from a walk. We got to know the school teacher and his wife on the way there. The house met our needs perfectly. We exchanged addresses and telephone numbers and told them we would be finishing the planting season at Whananaki in about three weeks. I was amazed that they were so trusting of us, that they only wanted a verbal agreement. Not even a bond was necessary. Our prayer was again answered. How gracious and loving is our God. We rejoiced again in the knowledge of Him carefully watching over us in every detail of our lives.

During the next three weeks of tree planting at Whananaki, there were two days of torrential downpour. The placid stream became a raging torrent of fast flowing water trying to escape to the sea. Water poured from the steep hillsides bringing down debris of leaves and small branches. The main stream of the creek brought logs which were either caught in the banks, or washed by the high waves back onto the beach. The area where the cattle had grazed was all covered by the overflow of muddy floodwater, especially when the full tide caused the water to bank back up the creek.

In spite of the rain and floods, we planted all the allocated trees in time for our return to Orewa. Before we left it was the beginning of spring and the kowhai trees were in full bloom. On one hill near where we had finished planting, the older kowhai trees were up to ten metres high and stood amongst other types of taller native specimens. Their yellow trumpet-like blooms were so spectacular against the deep green of the higher trees which grew around them. I admired them from a distance. They seemed to add a lovely touch of colour wherever they grew and flowered. However, I liked it best when I was able to walk among them and hold a bunch of their exquisite blooms in my hand. At the same time the tui birds would be close by feasting on the bountiful nectar from the yellow blossom, while a couple of wood pigeons also sat in the trees taking their share of God's sweet food source. The kowhai flowered for about four weeks. It's one of my favourite trees of New Zealand.

One day we were finishing the planting on a bank under and around several large pohutukawa trees. The road was above us and Lesley was working inside the boundary fence planting. She was under the shade of a mature tree that had grown fifty feet high with its trunk just outside the fence. Lesley was on her knees planting. The next day was a beautiful, calm, sunny day and we were over on another place where we needed to check on trees, we had planted a year before. It was time for our morning tea break. Suddenly there was the sound like a rifle being fired. For a brief moment everything was still and silent. Then that second in time was shattered by a loud cracking noise. Both our heads were turned in the direction from which the sound came. Two pairs of eyes watched a pohutukawa tree crash down with a woosh and a loud thump as it made contact with the ground. All was silent and still again. About an hour later, a visit to the site revealed the force at which the tree hit the ground. Thick branches had broken off and were embedded in the soil. Ten of the trees Lesley planted were obliterated and the fence was badly damaged. The stump now had red shards of pohutukawa wood sticking out, three feet from the ground. We both realised the tree fell on the exact spot where Lesley was planting the previous day. In every circumstance of our lives, we are totally in our Creator's hands. We gave thanks again for His protection. It's so assuring to know God tells us His unseen angels are here to protect us.

As time moved on, so did the change of ownership of the property. We were only going up when we thought the place needed some tidying up, or the trees needed to be sprayed around to keep the weeds down. Our work at Whananaki came to an end in 2010.

When we were back at Orewa we soon got used to going the extra distance to Army Bay. It was there that we went to the cottage we rented until our house was finished in November. I took responsibility for building the decks and doing some of the outside work to reduce costs. So, each day I was kept busy. We were delighted with our home when it was finished. It proved to be the perfect home for us for almost ten years.

Both Lesley and I found the most enjoyment, and satisfaction in our voluntary work in the several churches we were involved with since our teenage years. We did things together where we could, but were not afraid to help in the mundane task that needed doing. But, the opportunities to lead or teach in small groups and see the spiritual growth in our own lives as well as others, gave us thanks to God that He guided us on this path. We involved ourselves with Christmas and Easter programmes that Howick and Orewa churches put on. I personally was involved in the Eldership of these churches which were both growing and vital community churches. Lesley was an encourager, especially among the women. God had taught us so much with our roles in raising a family, the churches and in Scripture Gift Mission. It was such a joy to serve the Lord in this way. My task would have been impossible without Lesley's help and encouragement. Truly, the Lord was with us every step of our journey. All glory to Him.

CHAPTER 10

To finish this memoir, I want to take you on the journey of the latter stages of Lesley's beautiful life. This account was started six months after her death so the memories were not forgotten. If I was to give this chapter a heading it would deserve the title of 'Never Alone'.

We had been married forty-six years when we heard words from the oncologist we didn't want to hear. 'Lesley, the growth in your breast will have to be removed because it's cancerous.' He went on to explain the various types of cancer, and the options there were for treatment. He answered all of our questions thoroughly. We settled on a plan for the operation and following radiation treatment. It was all a new experience for us as neither had been in hospital for health issues before. We thought that the procedure would be a success, and the treatment to follow would ensure it.

God had the ultimate control. He was the one who guided us in our decisions, both great and small. He was the one who took us by the hand in marriage, keeping us safe and providing all our needs through the years. My life's motto is a verse I learned in Sunday School,

Trust in the Lord with all your heart; do not depend on your own understanding. Seek His will in all you do, and He will show you which path to take. (Proverbs 3:5-6 NLT)

As we travelled home in the car, we didn't need to say much to each other. Lesley had her eyes closed anyway. That evening she showered while I prepared a meal. Later she sat back in her chair and said, 'I have been thinking about what Ruben said today, and I am trusting his judgment on the treatment. I think the radiation treatment is better for me than chemo. We can pray that God will give him and his team the help and wisdom they need to treat me.' So, we did pray, as did our family and many others in our church and other churches.

The scheduled operation went ahead. Lesley was in the hospital for three days. A nurse came to tell her what to expect now that she would have to have a prosthetic breast. She explained everything to Lesley, including the name and telephone number of the lady in charge of the business nearest to our home. And the young, gentle and quietly spoken oncologist, Ruben, was back to examine Lesley before I took her home. He always spoke with a soft authoritative voice.

'As far as we can tell, we have removed all the cancer cells from your body, and with the radiation treatment, starting in a month or so, we hope it will knock out any that we may have missed. Go home and have plenty of rest, and we will introduce you to the radiologist who will work out a schedule for you. Any questions?' he asked.

'How long will each treatment take, and how long will the whole programme be?' I asked.

He then explained that each treatment would take about an hour, and Lesley would receive twenty-five working days of radiation procedure.

Christmas and New Year were only a fleeting memory for us. It was a good time together with all our immediate family including Maurice, Lesley's younger brother and their ninety-six-year-old maiden aunt. Lesley and I had taken care of Aunty Loie, particularly in the last ten years of her life since Lesley took on power of attorney for her. Loie was still a champion Rummikub player. Her mind was very sharp but her body wouldn't do what she told it to.

In March, the radiation treatment went ahead as planned. After the first two days, we got used to the routine and knew where to go and what to do at the hospital. Each week the receptionist would give us a different time for the appointments. It took us five or six hours till the time we would be home again each day. We had a lunch break and a walk in the park just down from the hospital. Lesley needed the exercise, but towards the end, when she was too tired, sometimes we skipped the walk. The stress level was taking its toll on her the closer it got to the completion of her treatment. But at last, we were on day twenty-five. This called for a celebration.

On the way in we had to pay a bill at the rest home where Aunty Loie lived. It would take us ten minutes longer but we gave ourselves enough time. Lesley was back in the car and I had driven two kilometres when she said in a very low voice, 'I am not feeling too well.'

'Do you want me to stop?' I quickly asked.

'No. Take me to the Red Beach emergency clinic,' she said in a very urgent voice while struggling to get a plastic bag from the glove box.

Even in her distressed state, she knew what to do because of her nursing training. I drove in haste towards the local emergency clinic. It was only five minutes away. I thought she was going to pass out. She was ghostly white. Her head rolled over to one side. I put a hand on her knee, as I often did while driving. It had always been in better times than these. This seemed to be the longest short drive of my life.

The staff rushed Lesley into a side room, put an oxygen mask over her face, called the doctor who came immediately and shut the door. I sat on a chair outside the closed door where I heard quite a commotion inside without hearing what was being said. It seemed like a long time before the fuss eased off and a nurse came and told me they needed to get Lesley stable before sending her to hospital because she had had a heart attack.

While walking beside Lesley as she was wheeled to the waiting ambulance, I told her I would go home, get her bag, have a quick lunch, ring the family and be with her in about an hour and a half. She was very sleepy. I told her again I loved her. My numbed mind followed the sound of the ambulance until it went over a hill some distance away. I pulled myself together and drove home.

When I arrived at the hospital Lesley's eyes were closed but they opened as soon as I moved closer. There were tubes to her arm and others to her chest to keep a record of her heart. She removed her oxygen mask. I gave her a kiss and held her hand instead of giving her a big hug that we both could have done with at that time. After all, we should be celebrating!

I waited with Lesley all that afternoon. She was in the critical care unit and was to remain there overnight. Our son, Richard came in and told us our eldest, Rosemary, was coming from Howick with Christine, our youngest. They were to be there at about 7 o'clock.

A hot dinner was waiting for me at Richard and Tania's place, which was twenty minutes north of the hospital. As we shared Tania's delicious meal their four sons were all anxious to hear about Grandma. It was quite emotional hearing the young boys pray for their Grandma's healing. I knew too, that Rosemary and Christine, their husbands and children, would have Grandma in their thoughts and in hearts, because they loved her so much.

It was dark when I arrived home from Richard and Tania's. I wandered about the house. There was heaps to think about. My mind was confused and my body tired and cold. Lesley always switched the electric blankets on, but she wouldn't be there tonight. I could not contain the pent-up sobbing that followed.

Eventually I went to bed with a hot water bottle for comfort and warmth. I listened briefly to the late-night news on the radio. Sleep was hard to find. My old grandmother, long passed, came to mind. She wrote to me in my single days and then to us both when we married and lived in Hong Kong. There were fifteen letters in total over a ten-year period. She always wrote the same few words from the Bible, often squeezed in at the bottom of the aerogramme,

The Lord said, 'I will never leave you nor forsake you.' (Deuteronomy 31:8)

For a few minutes, I meditated on the words my grandmother had indelibly planted in my mind, so long ago. With these words also came back, 'Trust in the Lord with all your heart and he will direct your path.' A peace settled. I was trusting in the Lord, knowing that he would never leave me, and he would always direct my way. There was plenty of warmth and I found great comfort from the Lord's words to me. They were just right. Could I have finished that day of celebration any better? It was past midnight. A new day had begun.

Lesley was still in the intensive care unit as I walked in the next morning. A nurse was taking notes from the readings of the monitors though Lesley was much more alert than when I had left yesterday. A doctor came in late morning and just after lunch the chemist came and talked about the different medication they were going to prescribe. At last we had a few moments to ourselves.

'You want to know my thoughts?' Lesley asked, 'The doctor told me it was critical yesterday that I went straight to the emergency clinic. I don't know how I knew, but God was certainly with us.'

I shared with her how the Lord had given me such peace the previous evening. Now we had time to smile as we thought of God being present with us and for us. We really had the very best kind of celebration this side of heaven – close fellowship and communion with our heavenly Father. Our hearts were filled with joy. That was our together celebration even if it was a day late.

It was five days before I could take Lesley home. During that time, there were all sorts of visitors from grandchildren with their parents, church friends and the pastor, hospital staff and the chaplain. Though Lesley was tired, I could sense she was getting better towards the end of her stay because she was observing the different reactions of the other three patients and staff who treated them. It was quite amusing at times. She was in her element but anxious to get back home.

Several weeks passed before Lesley returned to managing the household chores again which I couldn't do quite as capably. The family were a great help providing meals and visiting often. We came to appreciate our good praying church that cares for people's spiritual and physical needs. Over the next few months, Lesley gently picked up most of the things she used to do before her operation. We went to Taupo for a short break. Life was getting back to normal.

Her visits to see the oncologist were reduced to six-monthly routine check-ups. At the end of each visit, Ruben would give her another form for a blood test before the next appointment.

The new year arrived much quicker than it had ever done before. On the 10th of January 2014, Aunty Loie went to be with the Lord. She was ninety-seven years old and lived on her own after her father died in 1984.

By March of 2014 Lesley was almost back to normal health again. We were going for longer walks and she got her confidence back so she could drive again. I took over a couple of the tasks that she had previously done, especially hanging the washing out and getting it in. She had missed a fair amount of church activities earlier when she had the operation. Both of us were actively involved in the Easter art and craft show which reached out to just over a thousand people that year.

In August we took a short holiday in Paihia. We did a couple of day trips including to Kerikeri for lunch and on to the Marsden Cross which we had not been to before. We also saw again the old house that Lesley's great-great grandfather had built at Waihapu, opposite Paihia. He came to New Zealand as crew on a whaling ship in the 1830s. His grave is in a plot behind the old stone Anglican church in Paihia.

I had promised to help our eldest daughter build a deck during the last week of the school holidays in October 2014. Her two teenage sons were a great help. We stayed in our other daughter's house while she was away with her family. They lived quite close to each other in Howick. The last day of deck building was quite hectic. The final job was to return the heavy drop-saw, back to the garage where we stayed and pickup Lesley. Rosemary had invited us to stay for dinner. That evening my speech became all jumbled and slurred. I ate my dinner without saying much except yes or no. I didn't tell anyone that I felt something was wrong.

Before the hour's journey home, I asked Lesley if she would drive but she declined. I thought she wouldn't accept because she hadn't driven on the motorway or over the harbour bridge for almost two years. The Lord knew the circumstance but still I asked for his guidance and help. We arrived home safely and I went straight to bed.

The next morning, I told Lesley about my experience and she made an urgent appointment for me to see our doctor. She also packed a bag for me which she put in the car in case I needed to go to hospital. Sure enough, the doctor did send me straight to hospital. He rang the emergency department and told them we would be there in thirty minutes. I found myself waiting in the intensive care unit to be monitored and assessed. I was told that I suffered a mild stroke and would be moved to the ward soon. My speech, right arm, right leg and emotions were the worst affected. It was very difficult to stop from bursting into tears which would fall whenever anyone of the visiting friends or family, our pastor, or the nurses, would say some words of encouragement. I didn't know why at the time, but in hindsight it may have been a way to express thanks for their visit or kind words. In those early days, I was unable to express myself verbally. Before sleep found me, I would often have a quiet weep to myself as I thought of God, ever-present for Lesley and me, even though we were then temporarily separated.

There was so much I found I couldn't do. Concentration for any length of time was very difficult. Movements that were automatic to me before the stroke, now I would pause for a moment and think how to do them. Even taking a walk was difficult, because I had to tell my right leg what to do again. I couldn't pray or read the Bible for the first few days. However, I knew that many people were praying for me and Lesley too. The thought of the care of so many brought thankful tears to my eyes. This was not so bad in private but quite embarrassing in public, though most people understood.

I was in hospital ten days and would have been there longer because they wanted me to wait for a bed in the rehabilitation ward. I knew it was very tiring for Lesley and the family to visit each day, so I asked and was discharged. I was glad to be home again to good food, my wife's caring companionship, and peace and quiet.

There was a lot to think about when I arrived home as there were several projects on the go, before I had the stroke. The basics like writing, typing, spelling, conversation, digging the garden, or hammering nails, were all hard to do. They took so long and were very frustrating. It was like being a little boy all over again, especially with the hammer. I still haven't mastered that again. I missed being able to hand write and journal my quiet times and prayers.

All these things were on hold except for slow reading of the Bible and finding out what God was trying to teach me. It was nearly four months from when I came home from hospital that things started to come together. While this was going on, my loving wife was efficiently supporting and caring for me. Lesley soon learnt that, what I used to do pre stroke, only took an hour. Post stroke, the same job would take three hours. Or I may need to get someone else who could do the task for me. I learned that some people who have a stroke, think they can do more than they are able. I am one of them. It's the old sin of pride raring its ugly head.

We had lots of visitors. Our family and the church were so loving, kind and faithful. Some helped weed and plant the garden. Others came and talked and prayed with us. Slowly I got back into a more normal way of life. After three months passed, my local GP told me I could drive again. Lesley didn't think that was such a good idea at first, but she was more relaxed after a month of my driving without incident. The simple little things like putting the indicators on was something I had to learn again. I also took back the lawn mowing and other garden tasks. Living was at a much slower pace for both of us now.

It was November 2015, so we booked a caravan holiday at Papamoa, our favourite camp site. To our surprise this was not the quiet place we had often been to in the last forty years. Lesley loved those holidays by the beach.

Lesley's next visit to Dr Ruben was soon after we arrived home from our holiday. I noticed a lack in her energy levels and her desire for longer walks tapered off. We were walking on the flat areas more. It was a long way to Ruben's office, so we requested a wheelchair at reception. Ruben was on time and spent a little longer than usual with us. Lesley made a list of things that were troubling her. She questioned her medication and he changed one or two by writing out a script for them.

'I will make an appointment for you to come in Lesley and have an infusion. It will take about three hours. You will get a letter telling you when and where it is and it will be about the middle of February. Your blood count is not as it should be and this treatment should help that. And there is one other thing, you will need another CT scan and blood test before the visit in February. I will arrange for this to happen.'

Just prior to the hospital visit for the infusion, Lesley's blood tests and x-rays copies were sent to the doctor's office. We were told to wait to see Ruben after the infusion was finished. Eventually, Ruben came and led us through to a room which was not like his normal office. There were two chairs there and he got another for himself. I looked around the rather large storage-like place we were in.

'I wonder what we are here for?' I said, just before he came back with a chair, put it down and walked about six paces to shut the door. He took his file off a bench and sat down. It was the 25th of February 2016.

'You may wonder why I asked to see you today, but it was to update you on your treatment, Lesley. I am afraid it is not good news as the radiation treatment has not done the job we hoped for, and the latest blood tests show that the white blood count is still too high. The CT scan also shows that the cancer cells have spread throughout your body except for your brain which is a real blessing. We will continue to give you monthly infusions which should give you more energy. And, we could give you chemo treatment, but I don't think that would be any help.'

'I wouldn't want to have chemo anyway,' said Lesley.

'What is the prognosis, I mean how long do we have left?' I asked.

Carefully choosing his words Ruben replied, 'You'd be very lucky to see the new spring growth this year, or see September in, but I have been wrong before.'

The long calm silence was only broken when I said, 'Lesley and I have often talked about this. We have had a good happy married and satisfied life. Together we raised three children and now have nine grandchildren.' I paused to give myself enough time to drive back the pent-up emotion that was poised to break out.

Ruben took a box of tissues from the bench and handed it to us while asking us the question, 'Do you have any support nearby?'

Lesley said, 'Our family is very supportive of us and our son and his wife live about twenty minutes from where we are. Our daughters live about an hour away from us. Then we have a loving and caring church who will give us a lot of support too.'

'We will assist you all we can in the medical side of things.' Ruben said. 'I have written a full report and sent it to your GP. You can go to him to discuss your medication at any time. I would suggest also that you get in touch with the local hospice in your area. They will give you good support. And there is another thing. You will need to be very careful with your right hip and the bones above the knee. The CT scan shows they are very fragile but you tell me there is no pain in that area, only in the groin. I could book you in for a hip replacement if you want or you can leave it for now. You have a lot on your plate just now.'

Before he left, he handed Lesley a copy of the report he had written and asked us if we had any more questions. We didn't have, so he told us we could go home when we were ready. With God's help we would face this trial together, trusting Him, even without knowing what the Lord had planned for us.

'I'm glad we had Ruben for our doctor,' Lesley said as we stopped to get in the lift. 'He is just so thorough and does what he says he will do.'

I agreed with her, but the lift came just as she finished her sentence. We had company. My mind was still on Ruben. I wondered how he could cope telling people day after day what he had just told us. God puts special people across our path at just the right time. We didn't see Ruben again.

Before driving home, we had a cup of tea and a sandwich in the park. There, Lesley put things into perspective for me. 'I know God is able to heal me, but I want Him to be able to do His will in my life, that good and pleasing and perfect will of God, that Paul talks about in Romans 12:2. I don't know how long I've got or the tough times ahead. Ruben gave me about six months. That may be all the time God has allotted for me here,' she said.

'So, if people ask what to pray for, I'll tell them pray for God's peace and for His will to be accomplished in our lives,' I said.

'That's good,' she said.

'We are in this together and I will help you all I can, just like you looked after me when I had my stroke. It's amazing isn't it, how the Lord looks after us,' I said.

As we drove home, Lesley put the seat back and slept while I took time for reflection. I was amazed and encouraged at the way she accepted what was before her. Like all the trials and tests we faced before, this was another she was going into with trust and confidence in the Lord. She knew that He would give His love, His peace, and His grace to take her through this trial. I was glimpsing, yet again, my wife's deep trust and the love for Jesus, our family, our church and me. I always loved and admired these qualities in her life.

My trial was quite different from Lesley's. How was I to cope with the death of my life's love and my best earthly friend? Did I have to argue with God about what was happening to us? Would I be right to get angry at God for letting this difficult trial come our way? No. Definitely not. Our heavenly Father would never put us through trials which were too hard for us to bear. I will be leaning heavily on Him for His comfort and love that only He can give at a time like this. He never makes mistakes and sure knows what's best for my life. It feels as if God is constantly there to remind me that faith, hope and love, through Jesus, are always within my reach. They will last forever.

The weeks that followed were rather hectic with visits to the doctors, and home visits from district nurses, family and friends from church, hospice nurses, and our pastor who often popped in. Home care people came three days a week to give Lesley a shower and wash her hair. By this time, she was using a walking frame to get around the house.

It was the middle of March 2016. Lesley was going to bed at about 7 o'clock in the evenings now. I would make sure everything was right and in place if she needed it later in the night. I was so sad to watch her getting weaker. I rarely heard her lovely laugh now, but she didn't complain or cry, though she was often in a great deal of pain. Early in our marriage we had developed the habit of giving each other a hug, a kiss and 'I love you,' before we went to sleep. These were very special moments especially while we faced the unknown. It was me who shed enough tears for each of us after I had tucked Lesley in, kissed her again and left the room so as not to be seen weeping. I would busy myself until it was my bed time at about ten thirty and then, as quietly as possible slip in beside her.

On the 26th of April things were quite different. At the usual time, I helped Lesley into bed but while slowly lifting her legs she flinched and her whole body tightened.

'Wait,' she said, in a pain-ravaged voice, her eyes shut tight and her head hard back on the pillow. 'Just lower them very slowly.'

I did, but I could sense she was still in agony.

'I will see if the pain killers work well tonight, but they aren't yet,' she said.

I talked quietly with her while she relaxed and her grip on my hand loosened. At half hourly intervals, I checked on Lesley. Just before my bed time I crept into the room and was greeted by a tearful voice that said, 'John, you had better call the ambulance because I can't stand this pain any longer.' Her next dose of pain killers was still two hours away.

The ambulance arrived about twenty minutes later and administered a sedative to Lesley which eased the pain. The two officers wrapped and strapped her in a frame, carried her down the stairs to the ambulance and drove off to the hospital which was forty minutes away. I was there early next morning in time to see Lesley just before they were ready to wheel her away for a scan. In half an hour she was back again but looking quite pale.

I asked, 'How was it?'

'The pain was almost unbearable when they shifted me from the bed to the scan. I almost passed out. They were more careful when they put me back. I have a broken hip,' she said.

The nurse came to take her blood pressure and temperature. She told us that they would be moving Lesley to a ward soon and that another doctor would see her there. I walked behind the orderly as he effortlessly steered Lesley in her bed around the wide corridors and onto the lift to the ward by the window with three other beds. The doctor came and arranged a time for the operation early next morning. He gave her hope that all the pain would be gone after the operation. Lesley was under medication to stop the severe pain, but still her real suffering showed in her body language whenever she moved. Just occasionally her eyes would moisten and a tear would squeeze out. I had to turn away.

Two very happy Chinese nurses came the next morning to collect Lesley. They chatted away to us like old friends and set our hearts at rest. I went with them to the waiting room of the surgery. Again, they explained all we needed to know very thoroughly. I could feel the apprehension as I held Lesley's hand and I wondered what more she would have to endure. My words to her were, 'You remember what my Grandmother used to write, God will never leave us or forsake us.' I bent to give her a kiss and a brief smile lit up her face as they wheeled her away.

Four hours later I was back by her bedside where the nurse told me the operation had been very successful and Lesley would be awake again soon. It took only a few minutes for her to open her eyes. She looked around the room, then at me and said, 'I'm free from pain at last.'

This was to bring a whole change in Lesley's outlook. A few days after she came home, her walking frame and walking stick were put to one side. I would take her for a drive to Shakespeare park, where on her better days, she wanted a walk on the beach. It was as if Lesley was being 'led by still waters', that restored her soul as she marvelled at God's presence and creation. We could also watch the newborn lambs through binoculars from the comfort of our lounge chairs, but it was much nicer to drive over to the park and see them up close.

Those days came to a sudden end on the 10th of July. Rosemary, our eldest daughter, came on a pre-arranged luncheon visit with her husband. They came with food for lunch, fresh flowers, as always, and in time for me to go to church. She did this as often as possible. We were all blessed by these times as with all the family visits. Just after lunch, Lesley had gone back to bed and was asleep before the others went home. Poached eggs were one of her favourites for the evening meal. To encourage her to eat, it was served with her best china set, a small posy of fresh flowers and a hot cup of tea on a tray. We spent some time talking about different aspects of life, our children and grandchildren. Lesley inquired about church and her friends who always had a special place in her life. When I left she was sound asleep.

That night I was especially cautious getting into bed so as not to disturb her. At eleven thirty I was woken by Lesley's urgent cries, 'Please come and help me.'

It took me seconds to get to her side. She was sitting on a shower stool in the bathroom, doubled over looking down at the floor. 'My arms and legs won't work. I want to get back to bed,' she said.

'I will try and lift you back onto your walking frame,' I said, as I positioned the walker beside the stool.

But I couldn't lift her or move her enough to get her onto the other seat. We had always been able to help each other in the past. That was very hard for me to face. So, I wrapped Lesley in a blanket, called the ambulance, who came in about five minutes, and took her on another Sunday midnight journey to hospital. By Thursday they were ready to discharge her and wanted me to take her home. Neither Lesley nor I could face the drama of five nights previous. We requested another night in hospital so we could make arrangements for her to get palliative care somewhere.

This was a daunting task. I didn't know where to start. At about three thirty in the afternoon, I was on my way home praying as I drove. I was assured that God could and would do the impossible. I was to call in at Richard and Tania's place and fill them in on the latest on Lesley. Tania summed up the situation quickly and with my permission immediately phoned the rest home at Evelyn Page Retirement Village. They had one unit available for us to see. Before closing time, we secured a room in the rest home section of the village. It was wonderful to see how the Lord was working out His plan for us. I was able to tell Lesley, by phone, before she went to sleep, that she would be moved from the hospital about lunch time the next day, Friday, the 15th of July.

I was waiting at Evelyn Page as the ambulance arrived to deliver Lesley. Not long before I had been home to collect some of Lesley's things she requested and a few extras to make her room look more homely. Richard helped me bring in her favourite chair and some of Lesley's own oil paintings – scenes from some of our holidays. There were photos of our nine grandchildren at different stages of their lives. To welcome her, the staff had placed a big bunch of fresh flowers in the room. Only after she was properly settled, she leaned on her pillow, look around the room and said, 'This really is a lovely room. It's got everything I need.'

I asked the senior nurse if Lesley would get well enough for a short visit home. She told me that she didn't think that would be possible because Lesley needed full-time care now. In the second week of Lesley's stay I was shown a nice room that was kept like a motel unit in the complex, and was invited to stay. Meals were provided and that space was perfect for my needs at that time. It saved me the travel time which was about an hour for the round trip. But more importantly, I was close to Lesley and could be with her for most of the day.

Changes were also quite quickly happening in my own world. Since Dr Ruben told us Lesley only had a few months to live, I was praying about my future, especially regarding where I should live. The family were praying too and making some good helpful recommendations. When they saw the care and attention Evelyn Page offered, they all agreed that this would be best for me even after Lesley died. It was an easy decision for me to make and I signed up for a serviced apartment after talking it over with a local solicitor. Having kept Lesley in the picture of what I did, she then wanted to see where I would be living. It was while I was in the motel unit at Evelyn Page that I was able to take her in a wheelchair up to the third floor. I wheeled her into the empty space which had a bathroom, bedroom, kitchen/dining and lounge room combined. From the window, she was able to see the bowling green and the view of Silverdale in the distance.

'I'll be able to bring you up here to see the bowls, and through the binoculars you can see Richard's place. It should suit my needs very well, but I don't know where I will put my workshop,' I said jokingly.

A tired hint of smile cracked her lips open as she said, 'I like it very much. If you can put a couple of La-Z-Boy chairs there, a cabinet for the TV against that wall and a small dining table over here, yes, you'll be able to move around them with a walking frame when you get to be an old man.'

Her face lit up as we shared the light-hearted moment together, though the uncertainty of the days ahead, did not dim the memory of that fleeting moment. It was brief time when Lesley was satisfied that I would be in a suitable place when she went to be with the Lord. It seemed that this was what she was waiting for. Lesley was at peace.

On the third morning after she viewed my future pad, she went quietly to be with Jesus. I was sitting on a chair by her bed holding her hand. Richard was there too. Just before she left us, Lesley opened her eyes and fixed her gaze, first on Richard and then on me. There was peace and contentment in that gaze as without a word she took her last breath, closed her eyes and died. But God was there. True to His word and promise that says, 'I will never leave you or forsake you.' He instantly took her spirit or life, away from her body to a perfect place we call heaven. We sat in silent wonder and awe at what we witnessed.

I went home from Evelyn Page the next day and was alone at last. Things were quite busy for a few hours at the village and I didn't have much time for reflection. Pastor Murray came for a timely visit the following morning. We were talking about Lesley's life when I started to weep again. I suddenly stopped. He said, 'It's alright for you to cry.'

I was busy wiping tears away while saying, 'They were tears of self-pity and I don't want to go down that path, as it would be hard to come out from.'

This was a turning point for me. There were many more tears as our family felt the grief and loss of one who had a major role in our lives for so long. But for me, I am thankful to say, the tears were no longer tears of self-pity. The Lord is my comforter and counsellor. And yes, He is the very best. I was also assured through His word,

That nothing will ever be able to separate us [Lesley or me] *from the love of God that is revealed in Christ Jesus our Lord.* (Romans 8:39)

For now there is separation, but not from God's unfailing love.

The good hand of the Lord was with us guiding and helping in Lesley's funeral service and her burial, which was a family ceremony at the Wainui cemetery. Then followed the settlement of the sale of our house at Army Bay, together with the cleaning up the accumulation of ten years living in a comfortable home. The tremendous comfort, love and help of the whole family were some things I will not forget. It helped to make a smooth transition into Evelyn Page village where I have been happily settled since then.

On the 5th of August 2017 we met as a family at one of Lesley's favoured beaches, which she loved to walk along. Sometimes we walked hand in hand and other times she would break away to paddle in the cool water. Sometimes she would have a small grandchild to take for a walk. One of these, Asher, now nine years old, said to his mother, 'I can't believe it's a whole year since Grandma went to be with Jesus.'

For all of us, the year went so quickly, but it was quite therapeutic for us to be together, celebrating the life Lesley lived to please God. She did it, by not only her deep trust and love for God, but by showing that love to people whose lives she touched, everywhere she went. And Lesley would say, 'I'm looking only unto Jesus, as I onward go.'

www.ingramcontent.com/pod-product-compliance
Lightning Source LLC
Chambersburg PA
CBHW051559030726
47592CB00001B/365